Mark The Glove Boy

MARK
THE
GLOVE BOY

OR 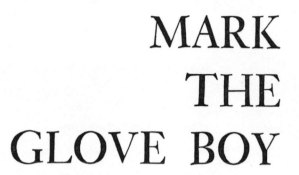 The Last Days

of RICHARD NIXON

By Mark Harris

The Macmillan Company, New York

Second Printing 1964

Printed in the United States of America

The Macmillan Company, New York
Collier-Macmillan Canada, Ltd., Toronto, Ontario

Library of Congress catalog card number: 64-14971

DESIGNED BY RONALD FARBER

The author wishes to thank Mr. Stanley P. Andersen and Mr. John McDonald for permission to reproduce their correspondence to him; and Mr. Irving Stone for his kind permission to reproduce a short quotation from his article entitled "The Tomorrow Country" published in *Life*, October 19, 1962.

for Ad Schulberg

Justice . . . to a hated man is possible only to a moral athlete.
—GERALD W. JOHNSON
in *The New Republic*

When you have a responsible job you've got to accept the responsibility.
—BIRDIE TEBBETTS,
manager of the Cleveland Indians,
in the Boston *Globe*

Knock knock.
Who's there?
Nixon.
Nixon who?
What, you forgot already?
—Children's chant overheard on
the streets of San Francisco,
circa December, 1962

Mark The Glove Boy

CHAPTER I ☞

       For a writer who has advanced beyond a certain stage of his life, the work itself is experience. No other reward awaits him. So at least it is with me, and so it was when the telephone rang—my old friend, the *Life* editor, from New York—though conceivably I weighed, in those first instants, as his voice poured into my ear, only the money he was at liberty to offer, or the strain upon my time. But now that the money has been spent, or squandered or saved or invested or taxed away and the time regained, the experience remains for me to convey, as I am about to do in the ironic form of a literary object exceeding in style the object I was commissioned to produce.

It was to be, my editor said, a California Issue, dated mid-October, and geared to the idea that California was to become, by surpassing the State of New York, the largest of the Union. Could I, he asked, contribute?—within, he meant, the limits of a prospectus then in preparation by the editors.

Of course. Why not? I keep open all the lines of my art. (I could always back out later and blame it on the poor prospectus.)

The prospectus, when it arrived, was a good one, lacking only what I knew beforehand it would—the negative tone, a strain of doubt, since it was true, and had been cleverly said many times, that Mr. Luce, proprietor of the magazine, thought of himself as the inventor of the Twentieth Century, and wanted us all to speak well of it. There were things in the prospectus I might speak well of. I might choose to report on the extensive educational system of the State of California; or, more narrowly, on the Board of Regents. Courteously rejecting those ideas, I suggested that I be allowed to retrace Mark Twain's travels through the state, but my editor said that the historical touch was to be provided by Irving Stone, as in a fashion it was, weighty in the way of fact, and scrupulous to avoid independent expression:

On June 27, 1776, a party that had come up the trail from Mexico pitched camp near the site of a mission they would build. The community would remain and become Yerba Buena and later San Francisco. The Los Angeles pueblo was founded in 1781 by 12 men, 11 women, 11 boys and 12 girls, comprising Spaniards, Indians, half-breeds, Negroes and one "Chino." . . . San Francisco, center of the gold wealth, was rapidly becoming a metropolis. In the short period of four years it boasted the addition of four theaters, 10 public schools, 12 daily newspapers, 18 churches, 20 foreign consulates, a water company, omnibuses and a public library of 3,000 volumes. The city had mushroomed to 50,000 inhabitants. . . .

In the end (to make short what's bound to be a long story) it was agreed that I should write about the gubernatorial race between Governor Brown and Richard M. Nixon. Of course, that was history, too, if I could make it so by seeing it with a distant eye down the wrong end of the telescope, seeing it as both a function of the recent past (from, say, the time of Christ) and as a portent for the future. Mr. Stone would make little of much, and I would make much of little, to give the Issue balance.

The decision was made by *Life*, not by me. True, I had suggested myself for the task, but I hadn't really expected to be entrusted with it. Offhand, I thought of myself as too prejudiced, too unreliable, seldom Olympian in an election year, and never Olympian with respect to Mr. Nixon. Accepting the decision, hanging up the phone, I expected any moment to hear the phone ring again, the project called off, word having got round the *Life* office to the proper party, who said, "No, not Harris for that; put him on something that matters less." But no such call came, then or ever, no instructions, no hints regarding preferences or favorites, no official *Life* position, not the remotest clue to Mr. Luce's secret thinking. The experience was to be wholly mine, after all.

I had taken the call from *Life*, not at my home in San Francisco but in a telephone booth baked by the sun at the Airway Motel in Nevada City, a little Californian mountain town where I vacation with my family. I was wearing bathing trunks, and about my shoulders a towel to protect me from flies during what would be a leisurely call of the sort *Life* makes at any distance, to the distraction of one who, like me, was raised to think of the long-distance telephone as the last line of defense against mortal emergency.

That evening, August 2nd, with my wife, three children, and our housekeeper, I left Nevada City by car, my intention being to enjoy a cool ride against the lowering sun: halfway home darkness would fall, the children would sleep, my wife and I would talk.

But we were less than halfway home, the sun still up, when an event occurred which was to color my thoughts during the next ninety days, as the gubernatorial campaigns progressed from their respective "kickoffs" to Election Day. Ten miles beyond Yuba City our Toyopet broke down, offering no warning, neither gasping nor faltering, its motor simply stopping, granting us only sufficient momentum to reach a shoulder of the road out of the path of the pursuing traffic, which, now, through the silence of our motionlessness, swept past us in a fury of speed and indifference as we adjusted ourselves to this new and frightening situation.

[4]

Near us was a small house. It appeared deserted. But when I crossed the road, I discovered that it was occupied by an old man and an old woman sitting in the gathering darkness, without lights, probably to conserve electricity, watching television, and loath to respond to my knock upon their screen door until a convenient moment occurred—a commercial announcement, I suspect, for in unison, at a break in the tone of the box, their bodies relaxed in their chairs, and in unison their heads turned toward me. The man laboriously rose and came forward. I described my plight.

But what could he possibly do? He had no telephone, no physical resources, and not even sympathy, for by contrast with him a man of my age surely needed none. Either out of habit, as a preparation for the night, or to punctuate our relationship, he hooked the screen door from within, and turned back to his wife, their television, and their darkness.

I recrossed the road to my car. My older children, who had already absorbed the idea of our peril, and in the same process discharged it, were seeking amusement at a safe distance from the road, though not so my wife, who knew by the swiftness of my return that I had accomplished nothing, and whose reason instructed her in the necessity for coolness even as her spirit must have urged her to chide a man foolish enough to attempt to maneuver California vastness in a Japanese car.

Our housekeeper, Mrs. Queenlee, sat as she had been sitting since we left Nevada City. Her habit of perpetual reserve was born of the discovery that words were seldom useful. Words build into theories, but to the profoundest theory—theories of child care, economy, hygiene, education—her polite response was always, "It's possible." In the momentary expectation of disaster she calls every child "Poor little thing." She was gazing forward now, as if still traveling, the baby asleep in her arms.

We had no night's supply of milk for the baby, no other food, no blankets, no water, no flares, no tools, and no mechanical aptitude. Our prospects compared unfavorably with the several days of comfort and abundance at the Airway Motel, all the more ironically in view of our present proximity to human help racing past us, but unlikely to stop, and less and less likely as the darkness deepened.

This spectacle of indifference first alarmed me, and then offended my senses, first accentuating my predicament, and then casting suspicion upon all mankind for its callousness, its speeding past the points of trouble, and its fear, too, of its own better impulses—for the motorist who stops may, after all, be repaid for his charity with a blow on the head. (Was *Life*, anywhere in its California Issue, prepared to accommodate this California moment, this fear? Would the colorful photographs of abundance reveal this subtler form of poverty? Would we see in *Life* those Two Old People in the Dark?)

If the motorist feared me, the suspicion was mutual: desiring help, I was also wary of it, a lone man at a lonely point of highway, not only without tools but without weapons. I have never owned a gun.

You may turn it around and ask, "Would *you* have stopped?" Yes, I have always stopped, fearing the blow I might receive for my trouble, but fearing more my shame

[6]

at not having stopped. My motives are impure. Surely they are less pure than the motives of the man who *did* stop.

He had no motive at all except the single motive of rescue, or if he had motives he could not have stated them—who might have said, had I speculated upon his motives, "It's possible," who, seeing our trouble, simply stopped, in spite of the difficulty of braking at the speed he was traveling, curving across the road at us, onto our gravel shoulder in his massive, ancient, beaten, powerful, roaring Buick whose doors flew open before it was ideally stopped, and whose occupants spilled out and surrounded us and without words or introduction poked their heads and lights beneath our hood.

They were boys, mostly, four or five of them, and one old man, and the driver, who was midway between the boys and the old man and who was also speaker and leader and whose decision it must have been to stop, for there could have been no time for consultation. The old man was his father, I think, or perhaps his uncle, and the boys were his friends and nephews, except one, who might have been his son or even grandson but was, in fact, the driver said, "my little brother," meaning orphan or waif or a sister's illegitimate child whom the driver had taken unto himself because the child was unwanted; taken him without motive, without any sense of service, out of impulse only, just as he had braked and stopped out of impulse, and chained our car to his and towed us ten miles to Yuba City, where, after small delay, our lives resumed.

There my story ends, its climax achieved with the braking and stopping. I do not know its hero's name. I have thought of him since as The Chain Rescuer, entering him into memory by that name, having no other, as I have no other for The Two Old People in the Dark. I remember the weathered, ruddy, inelegant redness of his face, almost its ugliness, and the smile he was obliged to carry so long as he carried such a face; and it seems to me The Chain Rescuer rescued not only my family and Mrs. Queenlee and me but the human race itself, just at the moment I had begun to view it as a hostile face at a speeding window.

He had started not only my car but my whole life going again, and I was to think of him in the weeks ahead, seeing faces like his in the crowds who came to hear the candidates. I am certain I saw his wayward sister shaking hands with the Governor in the cannery at Modesto, and again at the fairgrounds at Pomona where Mr. Nixon's campaign began, and I thought of myself as committed now in an unexpected personal way to return favor for favor, impulse for impulse: if I had been helpless on the shoulder of the road, he was helpless to defend himself against words. I would try to clarify for him, as surely as he had towed me with his chain.

Amidst the luxury of a *Life* assignment to two political camps eager to smooth my path—eager, even, to clarify the words *for* me and save me the trouble—the peasant face of The Chain Rescuer gave life to the abstraction of a public, a society, a voter to whom I owed exactly that responsibility often alluded to by the candidates themselves.

But it was only August, and I dared not crowd too fast a magazine article whose deadline was October and whose

[8]

principal quality was to be a validity carrying beyond Election Day, into the future. It should say something well and gracefully about Mr. Nixon and the Governor, but also about American politics, American life, and American feeling along the lines of a grand perspective.

I needed, then, to pace myself, to permit thought. As a boy I had often played too hard in early innings and so lost ball games to less exuberant boys plodding past me at the end. But now I was a man, and I had learned about pace. I ushered Mr. Nixon and the Governor to a corner of my thoughts, and bade them wait while I prepared my mind.

I knew my prejudices. The facts I could gather, but the prejudices I'd need to confront if I was not to be unfair to the posterity I modestly assumed I was writing for and to my own pride of craftsmanship, which had thus far guarded me against the error of writing today what I should lament tomorrow.

Mine would be the "lead" article in the California Issue. More California voters would read it than would read any other single campaign document except the ballot. Perhaps it would affect the outcome of the election. Something was demanding responsibility now in a way not demanded before, as when one becomes a father and seizes a power he never held. It was important to be just.

We had arrived home from Nevada City on a Thursday night. On Sunday, Marilyn Monroe was dead, a suicide, it appeared. I wasn't in the least surprised. I might have predicted it if I'd thought about it, having once written a story about a man who barked so brilliantly like a dog Hollywood would never cast him as a human: he too tried suicide. Several months earlier, commissioned to write upon the general subject of Women, I had ushered *them* to a corner of my thoughts, pacing myself with women as I was now pacing myself with the Governor and Mr. Nixon. I had been depending upon something to crack the case for me, and Marilyn Monroe's death was it.

For two weeks in August I went every day to the Public Library, where I read the newspapers and magazines as they touched upon Miss Monroe from her beginnings to her public end and sad burial. The articles about her purported to be new, fresh, exclusive, but as time went on and she became less public, less available, and more withdrawn, they began to feed upon themselves, seldom even troubling to disguise their plagiarism, while piously insisting (in stolen language!) that Marilyn Monroe's longing for escape was only a pose: with all her money and all her fame, how could she possibly be bored?

It seemed to me an old story in America of the career frozen at the moment of its awakening. In literature, one could name off the top of one's head a dozen men, past or present, torpedoed by their own success. I thought it might be the fact of Marilyn Monroe, and I began to think it might also be a political fact—specifically, the fact of Richard Nixon, for of course I was thinking of Mr. Nixon in the act of thinking about Marilyn Monroe.

She had failed to make her break. Of literary persons one might say that they, too, failed to make their break, failed to tell us all they knew. Perhaps Mr. Nixon planned to make a break and to tell us what he knew. Perhaps he wished to become a New Nixon. His place achieved, his power gained, why not a New Nixon in a manipulable setting, running free? Would he risk it, saying now or never, defying his supporters, a second career ahead? Perhaps he had some noble plan for himself, as Marilyn Monroe had but couldn't carry through, some intention to exceed himself and become what he had never been. I began to think of him in those terms, and I wanted to report him in that light if that was what emerged. I wanted to be sharp. I wanted to see him with my own eyes.

Put bluntly, I had come to identify with him at the expense of my old prejudices, as I identified with Marilyn Monroe, or with my barking man.

My friend Mark Linenthal—The Real Mark, he sometimes says—told me I should take a gun with me and shoot Mr. Nixon. I could carry a little silver revolver somewhere up my sleeve, cleverly attached by strings and wires to the important muscles of my arm, so that when, meeting Mr. Nixon, my hand should come forward to shake his, the revolver would spring out, I'd fire thrice and cry, "*Sic semper tyrannis!*" and flee.

But gunfire breeds gunfire, and we don't want that. I kept daily at the scrubbing of my prejudices. I read a thousand pages of The Achievements of Governor Brown, prepared by his staff; not neglecting to read, and more than once, since its bulk was less, Mr. Nixon's book *Six Crises*, prepared by Alvin Moscow, whom I was soon to meet. I gave equal time to each, an hour to this, an hour to that, my mind open, my attitude flexible, and my disposition agreeable. I was not only as neutral as I could be, but I managed even to set my mind against the Governor, beginning upon the principle that he had already been governor for four years. I had never met him, but my wife had sat at a table near him one day at Fishermen's Wharf, and she confirmed the general impression that he was something of a *bumbler* (the word commonly used against him), somewhat overweight, faintly ungrammatical, falsely friendly, and given to enunciating mighty principles in mixed metaphors.

I trained myself to counter good with good and bad with bad as I prepared my mind for work. If I went downtown to visit one headquarters, as I began to do the week before Labor Day, I did not fail to visit the other. They were located on lower Market Street, within a block of each other—Political Row one might have called it had there been more than two, or any permanence to them. Their proximity was less than accidental, arising from their similar mentality, the sworn enemies huddling together because the familiarity of enmity was at least warmer and more endurable than the cold aloofness of a public which, at this point, couldn't care less: California's two National League baseball teams, Giants and Dodgers, were embraced in a battle yet to ensue in a three-game playoff followed by a seven-game transcontinental World Series, interrupted by several days of rain, thus unnaturally extending baseball season past mid-October and diverting attention from political events already anxiously scheduled to avoid competing with the Liston-Patterson heavyweight prizefight. The afternoon of the only television debate between Mr. Nixon and the Governor was also the afternoon of one of the Giants-Dodgers playoff games, when thousands of Californians who might have watched the debate watched the game instead, with results impossible to calculate.

In my effort to begin without prejudice, I had at least the advantage of knowing the source of my . . . my what? I was about to say "politics," but it may be that I never had any politics, only hysteria. I can tell you the year and the night my politics or my hysteria began. It was twenty-two years earlier, in 1940, when the public world, innocent of Mr. Nixon and the Governor, was preoccupied by the race for President between Wendell Willkie and Franklin D. Roosevelt, Roosevelt trying for his third term and I on my first job, delivering gloves in big boxes for Meyers Gloves, then at Number One Park Avenue. The gloves were meaningless to me (I was afterward told they were fine and even famous gloves), but the boxes mattered because it was my job to carry them up and down the streets of Manhattan, on and off buses, in and out of subways to the truckmen's platforms of fine and famous department stores, where I was always treated with imperious contempt by captains of transport ordering me this way and that, go, stop, pickup, deliver, shove, push, wheel, carry, load, unload, and above all stay out from underfoot. Those were cold days, the winds flailed me in the canyons, and my hands froze because, though I was a glove boy, I was saving my only pair for Saturday night.

The worst moment of the job was the last chore of the day, my wheeling a handcart at evening, in the lowering dark, at the height of the rush hour, to the post office several blocks away. The rule of the shop was that this was a two-man job, for the cart was heavy; when loaded it was badly balanced, and the man pushing (assuming one was pulling) pushed blind, for he had no visibility behind the boxes. The partner to whom I was assigned disliked this chore and was unfit for it. He was the least healthy man I had ever known, his gauntness painful to behold but beyond remedy, since he was allergic to almost every variety of food, subsisting upon saltine wafers, which he swallowed with effort, gasping and choking, his eyes watering. By the end of the day his exhaustion was total. Though he left the shop with me each night, he never accompanied me to the post office, wordlessly staggering away, leaving me alone with the gloom before me, at the hind end of my unmanageable handcart, amidst the cursing of cabdrivers and the snarling of policemen.

Clearly I was of the working class. Yet, in spite of this, because my father was, I was a Republican, his politics or his hysteria mine. I wore a Willkie button. I remember a certain man who said to me on the subway, as I was traveling for Meyers Gloves, "Wouldn't you think a Willkie button could afford a taxicab?"—complaining in a single question of both the space I required and my politics, though it was the politics he more deeply felt. Nor was the clever double edge of the question lost upon me, young as I was (not yet eighteen), for I carried a book of poetry even among the gloves, and I knew something of the ways of words. I knew I was incongruous, and I didn't want to *be* incongruous, though I didn't know how to stop. I was already resenting incongruities, false claims, cynical piety, the habit of doing one thing while saying another. I knew, in spite of my father's explanations, that my fifteen-dollar salary would have been less but for the eight years of the New Deal.

And I knew, in the stockroom at Meyers Gloves, that I was making poor arguments for Republicanism and Wendell Willkie. I was making little headway among my fellow workers, who were all for Roosevelt, who jeered at my suburban beginnings, and who linked my peculiar politics to my peculiar habit of carrying a book. I was out of things, set apart. It was a scene I would eventually understand.

One day in October I offered myself for work to the Willkie headquarters in Mount Vernon, New York, my home city. Of course, it was volunteer work, after hours. I typed long lists of names. No doubt my lists proved useful, but the people among whom I worked, though I had known them all my life, suddenly began to appear alien to me, even as the glove workers, though alien to me at the beginning, had begun to appear less so. Among these Willkie workers, who were engaged in a great crusade to save the nation from Roosevelt's tyranny, I began to know a mysterious fear and mistrust.

Since I could not name what I feared and mistrusted, I went doggedly on until, on a certain night late in October, a truth came to me. On that night Mr. Willkie himself delivered a major address (not quite in Mount Vernon, for no such honors ever came to us) at the Empire Race Track, as it was then called, in nearby Yonkers. I was selected to be an usher. I wore an armband to match my Willkie button. We were ushers by the hundreds in a crowd of thousands, our duties vague and unspecified, the whole rather disorganized, and the work force far exceeding the job to be done. (Such a waste of man-power would never have been permitted at Meyers Gloves.) I ran desperately from one official person to the next, complaining of my unemployed energies, but little could be found for me to do. Many of the other ushers complained in the same way.

Much later—twenty-two years later, at the Nixon kickoff at Pomona, California—I was to realize that what had been wanted was not our labor but our cheering, not our ushering but our noise, our excitement, our enthusiasm, and our bulk. It was this that would rally others, and rally, too, I suppose, the candidate himself, though he must have known that the noise was spurious and his cause probably lost, for in 1940 the united glove workers of America were in no mood to surrender new rights to a Wall Street businessman. As for me, however, I had no idea that the cause was lost. No cause was ever lost in those young days, and though the enthusiasm of others may have been manufactured mine was not, and I cheered until my throat caved in—until it simply refused to function, a phenomenon dating from early childhood, when I went hoarse every year at summer camp, my throat having learned, apart from me, to refuse to be abused.

But the more lasting truth of that October night at the Empire Race Track was counted out for me in the faces of certain citizens of Mount Vernon gone to Yonkers, a pattern that troubled me: for they seemed to be, by and large and with fearful regularity, almost everybody I had ever associated with anti-Semitism. For a Jewish boy living through the era of the zenith of Nazi power, with nothing but the Atlantic Ocean lying between Yonkers and Hitler Germany, this parade of real or imagined anti-Semites down the aisles of the Empire Race Track would be a fact of ultimate importance.

For better or for worse, wisely or unwisely, my politics were born that night. I supported Mr. Willkie to the end, typing his lists, wearing his button, bitterly regretting his defeat, and vowing to support him again and forever, however often he ran. But alas! By the time of the next presidential election he was dead, Roosevelt ran for a fourth term, and I cast my virgin vote for the man who appeared likely to become the permanent President of the United States. The seeds of this defection had been planted on that October night when I had begun to feel, in the gravest corner of my heart, that love and loyalty for Mr. Willkie and the Republicans might require reexamination, restudy, for in some dim or indirect manner, but nevertheless actual and real, Mr. Willkie was dependent upon supporters alien to me.

Was it hysteria? Or was it reason? Whatever it was, it was within me twenty-two years later, going up in the elevator to the Nixon headquarters on the other edge of the continent. It was mingled with my will to be fair to him. Twenty-two years of my own growth, my own shifting identification, would give it (I hoped) equilibrium.

Here I would establish my first live contact with the Nixon forces. Of course, I was hoping that all things would be beautifully different now, that the choice would lie between two equally benevolent forces. I was prepared to believe that twenty-two years had worked marvelous changes, thrilling reweavings of the social pattern no less spectacular than the shift of my own identity from glove boy to *Life* correspondent.

As far as I could tell, on my first glimpse beyond the Nixon door, it amazingly had. The girl at the switchboard was reading a book. I couldn't see what, but it was no frivolous book, no lending-library novel, and since she had little real control of the switchboard I suspected that she was a volunteer worker, and I took hope from the thought that Nixon volunteers read good books. But No, she said, she wasn't a volunteer; she was a paid worker. "Then you're not," I said, with some disappointment, "a passionate Nixonite." "You don't have to be passionate to run a switchboard," she replied, meaning, I took it, that she wasn't saying Yes and wasn't saying No; meaning, I took it, No, she wasn't, passing through to the inner office of the lady I had come to see.

My lady had a title and a name. Both escape me now. She was director of public relations for Northern California, my liaison, my connection, so to speak. She was a stocky, professional sort of woman, giving me the impression of a tailored suit and short hair, though it might have been otherwise, eager to be helpful, but somewhat doubtful what her attitude ought to be toward the press, wanting to be cordial without losing her dignity. Toward me she was particularly doubtful, as person, apart from press; there was confusion here: having been announced to her by the passionless girl as "Mr. Harris of *Life*," I was quick to tell her, the instant we met (for I'm no politician; I burn to keep the record straight), that I wasn't really "of *Life*," that what

[18]

I really was, or really was *of* . . . well, I could hardly say.

My relationship to the campaign was to be of this confusing character, all to prove to the good in the end, for in the end it was my definition in the eyes of others which would force my identity upon me, force me to act it out, heckling me into being who I most truly was, and thereby producing my most useful and illuminating moments with Mr. Nixon, giving me my truth of him, and my story to tell. Perhaps my not being "of *Life*" was *Life*'s reason for choosing me: fresh to political reporting, requiring nothing of Sacramento, I had no favorite politicians, none had me, there were no debts either way, and no old friends to serve. True, I had an emotional past which was bound to define a political present, but that couldn't be helped; everybody had one; it was how I handled it that counted, how I'd rise above it by consciously knowing it and what it looked like and whether it ruled me or I ruled *it:* it was all in knowing who was boss, my past or I.

So my lady might have asked, "How can I help you for my cause if I don't know who you are?" She began by presenting me with pamphlets and brochures of every sort, often adorned with photographs of Mr. Nixon, or of Mr. Nixon and Mrs. Nixon, or of Mr. and Mrs. Nixon and their daughters, or of persons endorsing Mr. Nixon, and with slogans and mottoes trying out for places in his campaign, asserting his honesty, his sincerity, his will to win, his capacity for work, his decisiveness (Mr. Nixon's *decisiveness* would be a big campaign theme), his distinguished career of public service, and many details of his past; and she promised to place my name on all the mailing lists, though that wasn't what I wanted, as I demonstrated by taking all she gave me and sliding it unexamined between the pages of my Emerson—the essays in the red Rinehart edition, which I carried with me, preparing for my semester in American Values; he who would sometimes be, or so it seemed, my only companion in the weeks ahead, whose consecutive logic and high style would be my sole consolation, my lifeline to civilization, my protection against the avalanche of political language, my assurance that somewhere a humane society still existed, my fresh air, wings and lungs for my drowning brain, aristocratic wit amidst a touch too much democracy.

Then what *did* I want? Lifting her telephone, my lady called a man whose voice replied from the other side of a thin partition, and who soon came with more pamphlets and brochures.

As often happens, what I learned I learned by the way, not by asking, nor by being given. I happened to mention seeing a storefront advertising itself REPUBLICANS FOR BROWN (the same sort of vacant store in which I had typed for Willkie in Mount Vernon, New York). "Oh," she said, "some Democrats claim so. It's only Democrats." Yet, she had had full faith moments before in DEMOCRATS FOR NIXON. I soon learned to guess accurately at the truth of things by studying not claims but accusations. It was a good tool to discover early; it led eventually to a clear view of the political mind in general, and Mr. Nixon's in particular, which knew so little about itself, or, knowing, failed to understand.

A second discovery was of the passion of the Nixon

camp. My lady was passionately for Mr. Nixon. Everybody in the Nixon camp was passionately for Mr. Nixon. The only known exception was the girl at the switchboard. Possibly it had to be passion or nothing, and possibly, in the end, it was the passion that undid him. His complaint, in the beautiful and righteous fury of his Farewell Address, echoed his complaint after 1960 against his own people for their failure to get out the vote. By the act of blame in 1960 he enforced passion in 1962. But the Nixon worker might have done better, stayed looser, had he been freer of his passion. Stressing decisiveness ("Give California a Decisive Leader"), deploring doubt or hesitation, Mr. Nixon was rewarded by a passion not unmixed with fear. It was not a good atmosphere for flexible, relaxed labor, independent thought, the exchange of ideas, free speech. I thought of Japanese warships said to have been sunk, with all hands drowned, because speech was frozen belowdecks for lack of the language to transmit orders up.

If Mr. Nixon was like a Japanese naval commander, the Governor was like the man with the boy and the donkey, tending to listen to everyone—first riding the donkey; then, under criticism, permitting the boy to ride; then both riding; then both at last carrying the donkey. The passion of the Governor's people was mingled not with fear but with amusement, his people smiling at the mention of his name, as if his importance was considerable without being overwhelming. Nobody was awed by his presence; nobody stuttered and trembled; people told him freely how they felt about things he had done, where he was wrong, where he was right, he himself often inviting this exchange by concluding statements with a little inquiry I learned to anticipate and admire: "Don't *you* think so?"

Was it that that was meant by people who called the Governor indecisive? I had begun by trying not to like the Governor, as I began determined to like Mr. Nixon, for the sake of equalization, but the Governor's little question, with its charming implications, tended to subvert my intention. I never heard Mr. Nixon ask anybody anything.

According to my rule of equality, I was at pains to pay my first visit to the Governor's headquarters on the same day I had visited the Nixon headquarters. On the stairway I met two ladies, and in my quest for real differences between the candidates I studied these ladies of the Governor's staff, comparing them with ladies I had met up the street at the Nixon headquarters. I wanted to make something of them, without making too much. I wanted to make something of everybody and everything, but not too much: I was still pacing myself, still hoping to avoid commitment, as an actor, I am told, often avoids mastering his character too soon, lest he master it wrong. I did not know these ladies, but I thought I knew the *type*. I had met them somewhere, protesting something somewhere, or perhaps at a co-op children's nursery. What was I to make of these ladies there upon the stairway? What did they symbolize, if anything? "Symbols are what fly off everything," said Robert Frost. What was flying off these ladies? I asked if anyone was above, and they looked at each other, not quite remembering. They didn't know. I could go above and see for myself.

The headquarters was almost deserted. I could have stolen

it blind. I was particularly sensitive to the typewriters, alone and unguarded, my impulse being, when I see a typewriter, to steal it, a reaction dating back to my early working days, my life as a glove boy when, burning to write but owning no typewriter, I borrowed one when and where I could, working always in those old days against the deadline of an owner—a friend, a hotel clerk, a boss—who might at any moment return, reclaim his machine, and by interruption abort my masterpiece. When the time came that I was able to afford a typewriter of my own, I bought not one but several, and I could never part with one, even after its parts had been pounded useless, couldn't sell it, couldn't give it away.

I made what I could of the free, open, unguarded space of the Governor's headquarters. I tried not to make too much of it. It may have meant nothing, though of course it may have reflected the personality of the Governor, things unlocked, unguarded. Or it may have meant money, for the Democrats behaved as if they had money. For example, though the traveling press was to have been billed for transportation expense, and though the Republicans billed me promptly, the Democrats never billed me at all. Or—small thing, perhaps—there was the hot day at the motel in Modesto when I carelessly said I'd not mind a swim but I'd forgotten my suit, and a new suit appeared on the bed of my room, its price tag torn away.

I might have turned and gone back down the stairs except that, having recently quit cigarettes (soon to resume), my acute nose smelled a cigarette burning in a distant office occupied, as matters turned out, by John McDonald.

[23]

McDonald, on leave from the San Francisco *Examiner*, was to be my chief source of Democratic information during the weeks ahead. We had never met, but he was acquainted with some of my writing, and he had recently seen me on television—an educational program he hadn't heard well (he was hanging drapes)—which impressed him as important, not for what I might abstractly have said at the time, which didn't much matter, but only for my being there, which did, not the substance but the notoriety.

Later, during suspenseful October days, after my article had appeared, my neutrality had been relinquished, and my hysteria had regained eminence, we were to talk several times on the telephone, not in the way of business (for by then we would no longer have any) but toward the end of mutual comfort, cheering each other up, and searching out the bright side of things as Election Day drew near.

My relationships with newspapermen soon badly deteriorate. Our conversations never go far before we clash. But I'd need the facts, the figures, the data McDonald, from the Democratic standpoint, would happily supply, and I wished to avoid his having to supply them to someone he didn't like. To disguise my antagonism I immediately became falsely hearty, lapsing into all my old assumptions about newspapers, asserting their necessity, their importance, in the very language of my young manhood, when I, too, had been a newspaperman, yet to be saved by the grace of God, hearing in my voice the words and tone of a time of my life remote and distasteful to me now, scooping up all the pamphlets and brochures he gave me, not with indifference, not slipping them unexamined into my

[24]

Emerson, but quite as if I thought them crucial material to possess.

The greater my appreciation, the greater McDonald's eagerness to supply me. Soon my arms were loaded, and we went downstairs for more. I so beautifully concealed all hostility that when we parted I could see he was rather pleased with me.

How would I manage, in the days ahead, with no companions but newspapermen? I knew them well. My life of work had proceeded—after the gloves, after the Army— as a newspaperman, boy reporter for the *Daily Item* in Port Chester, New York. It was a glorious year, but in retrospect a horror, a death I might have died. Later, I worked on newspapers elsewhere, to gain money to put me through college, but it was my Port Chester year that counted by telling me enough to imagine the rest. It is all reported in a book published before I was born, for Port Chester, New York, is *Winesburg, Ohio*, and I was George Willard, "running about and getting little items to print," so young that everyone talked freely to him, thinking he would scarcely hear, and though it was true that he didn't hear much he heard enough to know at last, by the sheer weight of it, that everyone was urging him to flee, to escape.

Port Chester is, or was, a somewhat shabby little city (Village, technically) diminished by wealthy and fashionable neighbors—Rye, Greenwich— cut through the heart by the noise of the railroad, and intermittently flooded on its flanks by the undistinguished Byram River. Port Chester offers the delightful aroma of Life Savers, which it manufactures, and of the Paul Arnold Brick Oven Bakery, behind the *Daily Item* office where I often wrote late at night on a borrowed typewriter, sometimes interrupted by someone knocking at our glass door, who proved to be a citizen in memorable distress, like citizens who knocked late at night at the door of the Winesburg *Eagle* to tell George Willard of events—to tell *me* of events—not quite, as I must have said, news, not quite in our line, not quite what we like to publish in our regular daily family newspaper. These events to which I was made privy had their meaning in another style, at another level, scandal unreportable because so ordinary, so usual, commonplace disappointments and delusions, memories and betrayals, miscarriages of justice attributable rather to God's will than to any living corrupt institution. Therefore they fell within no category of journalism.

I worked there exactly one year, intending to begin a second and an indefinite number thereafter, and would have done so had I not, on the afternoon of the first day of the second year, been forcibly struck by the limitations of what I was doing. I was sitting in the high-school grand-stand in the sunshine of a May day, listening to the marching band, which I had listened to a year before, and praised for its color and beat and enthusiasm, but which I could not praise again the second year, having learned too much in the year intervening.

The meaning of something said to me by another reporter suddenly seized me and illuminated me. He was one who drank on his beat, slept at his desk, and soon died, from whom I borrowed a pair of overshoes still in my possession when he died, and which I wore for several years thereafter with his name still inked at the instep. He had taken a bright little item, something with meaning, and written it as if it had none, missing the point in the Irving Stone manner. I said it might have been done better, and he replied, "When you've done it as long as me, you won't do it any better."

Now I knew the truth of what he said; in a single year I had wrung the experience dry. Nothing better was demanded. The meanings I had begun to attach to events were meanings no newspaper cared for; the symbols I began to see flying off everything were visible only to me and to a few eccentrics of that Village. The style of writing I hoped to develop—good, full, rounded sentences producing good, full, rounded thought—as an accommodation to my meaning was in excess of the style the newspaper required, since it didn't need the meaning to begin with. Moreover, I had learned to write more slowly, thinking more, when what a newspaper needed was not thought but speed. The faster I grew, the slower I went.

Of one contribution I was especially proud. I gave expression to certain sympathies then forming for Negroes, whose activities I turned to news, no doubt seeking it with greater energy than I sought mere white-man's news. (I was a member of the N.A.A.C.P., Port Chester Branch.)

In this I received much encouragement from my editor, one Edward Hughes. He knew nothing, I think, of my affection for him. He was a stern, fluent man, with an amazing fund of invective, who insisted upon scrupulous reporting within the limits the newspaper set for itself. He had what then seemed to me the occult quality of bringing my prejudices to my own attention, though he may have been more tolerant of his own—family and property values, the

Catholic Church, and the Republican Party. In many ways, physical and other, he bore a close resemblance to Governor Brown of California. He had many daughters. Perhaps I was a son to him. He admired my political fervor without sharing my convictions, tolerated my Roosevelt button in 1944, knew my sources, knew my impulses, encouraged me, applauded me, and forced me to merge my passion with my craft: scolded me, berated me, threatening with everything except dismissal, knowing, I suppose, that I should soon enough dismiss myself.

Fifteen years later, passing near Port Chester, I telephoned him. I imagine he had a cigarette in his mouth, and ashes falling down his chest. "Do you remember me?" I asked.

"Oh, my boy," he answered, "how could I forget you? You left your mark on Port Chester."

I was astonished. Years before, boarding the train and departing more or less forever, like George Willard, I had been certain of nothing so much as my failure. The possibility that I had succeeded did not occur to me until the moment his voice implied it, whereupon it became not only a possibility but a fact.

Now, in the autumn of 1962, in California, I was reporter again, assigned to cover Mr. Nixon, whose political life or death was a matter of some moment to America, as the political life or death of a Trustee of the Village of Port Chester had been a momentous matter, at least to him, and to me, and to Port Chester, when I was there. I had had my preferences in those days, favoring some Trustees above others, but if I had ever thought to cheat in writing of their actions I had always been checked by the living presence of Edward Hughes, hovering above the words I wrote, tearing them through with his black pencil, sending them back to me with marginal memoranda attacking my bias, until I learned the difference between the right way and the wrong way.

Could Mark The Glove Boy, for all his effort to subdue his hysteria, keep an open mind? Or would Mark The Glove Boy go with his little silver revolver up his sleeve? Perhaps the best I could do would be to live with my mind in the knowledge of its involuntary character, making allowances for it, making corrections for it, in the light of its known imperfection.

Think of my temptation, having left my mark on Port Chester, to leave it now on the whole United States. What a splendid opportunity, just this once, in the matter of Mr. Nixon, to falsify—I wouldn't lose a single friend—to "give him the shaft," as he afterward expressed it.*

And wasn't America ambitious to permit a glove boy such latitude? The marvel of it all was reflected in a letter from a friend beginning his second year of teaching in Finland, received in San Francisco the morning I left to meet Mr. Nixon:

* "I believe in reading what my opponents say and I hope that what I have said today will at least make television, radio, the press, first, recognize the great responsibility they have to report all the news and, second, recognize that they have a right and a responsibility if they're against a candidate, give him the shaft, but also recognize if they give him the shaft put one lonely reporter on the campaign who will report what the candidate says now and then."—Mr. Nixon, in the *New York Times*, Western Edition, Nov. 8, 1962.

Classes are about to begin again and I feel a little less odd conceiving what to say about Puritans and Natty Bumppo and Sweet Betsy from Pike in this clime than I felt last year. In fact I feel rather at home going to Hallituskatu . . . where the humanities building is and saying "Päivä!" right and left to students I recognize as I walk in—just as if it's perfectly natural that a Mormon boy who used to pitch hay should be discoursing on America. . . .*

* Stanley P. Andersen, San Francisco State College, from Helsinki, Sept. 6, 1962.

CHAPTER 2 ☞

                    Having read equally about each man, and having equally visited each headquarters for equal periods, I had hoped to make my first personal contact with each candidate at equal, comparable moments. Therefore I chose the moment of the kickoff to each campaign—Mr. Nixon's at Pomona in Southern California, near his birthplace, near his boyhood, near his father's grocery store, all rich with symbol and sentiment; the Governor's at Union Square in San Francisco, though the Governor would be less sentimental about it all, confessing that there were Oh, several kickoffs, in several places, symbols and sentiments sufficiently numerous to give at least several groups of party workers the sensation of being present at the origin of things, as at a ship's launching, although, as we all know, the ship has first been launched in private to see if she will float. Since politicians, like shipowners, arrange their ceremonies as much for the sake of publicity as for the love of God or man, photographers are welcome guests, aiming and snapping at everything standing or moving, inescapably producing printable pictures, as, it is said, ten thousand monkeys at ten thousand typewriters for ten thousand years will inescapably produce *King Lear*. I was to see a stupendous variety of cameras.

My own tools were less precise: pads of California Legal paper, with blue lines and a margin of doubled red lines down the left; a supply of ball-point pens; much of both; indeed, a great excess of both. I neurotically oversupply and overequip myself, for fear of running short—frightened when a boy, no doubt, by the advertisement featuring the despair of a man whose fountain pen ran dry at the critical juncture of a big business deal, though I have since wondered whether a deal so tenuous might not have been unsound from the start. In anticipation, I numbered the pages of my California Legal in each upper-left-hand corner.

At the top of the first page I wrote *a vision of the end*. I wanted to learn from each man what he thought life should be like beyond Election Day, next year, next century, in history. Had he even thought about it? Was God with him, or was His name simply upon his lips? Of course, I didn't intend to *ask* it in the manner of an interview, but to ask other things, and to listen for the style, tone, language, innuendo, and assumption of the reply: the *act* of reply.

I wanted not only to ask but also to eavesdrop at happy moments when each candidate was least aware of me. When, for example, a candidate was assisting photographers, and his mind was on the lens . . . ah, it was *then* that he often spoke most candidly, supplying the furtive listener with his truest evidence.

I wanted to listen to what *they* said, not to what their prepared addresses said they said, nor to what their headquarters said they intended to say. I wanted to see their eyes when they said it, and I wanted to see what they did with the sweat of the voter's palm after it had passed to theirs. I wanted to hear, not in their big talk but in their small talk, whatever escaped phrase might lead me to either man's truest sound, his areas of easy or uneasy conscience, what he talked about—or declined to talk about—when the option was his. I was determined that nothing be put over on me. I was the personal representative of The Chain Rescuer, The Two Old People in the Dark, Mrs. Queenlee, and my family; I was a voter myself, and I did not intend to be made a fool of.

Almost immediately my plan for equal treatment suffered a setback. I had gone to the Governor's kickoff in San Francisco without having first met him, but though I went to Los Angeles with the best intentions I could not resist an invitation to meet Mr. Nixon the night *before* his kickoff. In the long run it was profitable, and no harm done. It was to be a party, and I always learn much at parties by avoiding liquor and by rushing off periodically to the bathroom, whipping out my California Legal, and writing down all sorts of little tidbits which have overspilled people's cups.

The invitation had come at lunch that day in Los Angeles with Alvin Moscow—"Special Assistant to Richard Nixon," said his business card, displaying a familiar golden shape labeled N-I-X-O-N, spelled, on most other maps, C-A-L-I-F-O-R-N-I-A. Moscow had reached me first by letter, offering me "an earful of background, strategy and plans for our campaign," asserting, in the same letter, his admiration for *Wake Up, Stupid*, thus bewildering me, as I am often bewildered, by the happy capacity of many readers to receive pleasure from my impudence even in the act of supplying me with fresh material.

I soon deduced that Mr. Moscow had not read my book really well (it was just another book among many), for he was astounded by the careful manner of my reading *Six Crises*. He seemed to say I had taken the words too much to heart (I had even studied the footnotes!), that a book was not to be held responsible for the words it contained. He told me, in a tone of awe, that Mr. Nixon had written one of the six chapters *entirely* by himself, as if that fact rescued Mr. Nixon from any possible charge of having employed a ghost-writer.

Mr. Moscow argued at lunch (it was a friendly lunch, a friendly argument, not even an argument, really: I had gone to be convinced, to be brainwashed, to be argued out of all past prejudice; for an earful) that Mr. Nixon had, after all, gone back over the text of *Six Crises*, converting Mr. Moscow's style to his own, giving the whole his own character; that Mr. Moscow himself, between the outline and

[34]

the published version, merely supplied the prose which gave bulk to the structure.

I said I gained no sense that the writing of the chapter Mr. Nixon *did* write had been a crisis of discovery for Mr. Nixon; beyond that, I gained no sense from Mr. Moscow that the collaboration had been a crisis for either man—that one's autobiography is always, after all, more or less written by somebody else.

I suppose we ought to be accustomed by now to this deterioration of ancient definitions, that we ought not to be shocked. I suppose I should not have been shocked—perhaps what shocks me is our immunity to shock. Granted, we cannot all be writers, any more than we can all be actors or mechanics, or dentists pulling our own teeth; and yet, poor as our powers of expression may be, it is better that they be ours than be a hired expression, especially when, as in politics, we offer our expression as a sample of our character.

Writing is discovery, like thought or psychoanalysis, whereby the writer in the writing exceeds and overruns his outline. We may come to truth by discovery.

Or was it possible that Mr. Nixon, desiring no discovery, had decided in advance the discovery he wished to make? It was not Mr. Moscow but another of Mr. Nixon's staff, Steve Hess, who, with a pride all unwitting, afterward answered this question for me. "He decides the position he wants to take," Hess told me, "and we find the facts for him."

The party to which Mr. Moscow invited me occurred at Mr. Nixon's home in Beverly Hills—up in the hills: you couldn't get there except by car. I arrived early (another neuroticism, like oversupply), long before Mr. Nixon made his appearance, thus affording myself the opportunity to describe his house on my California Legal, to think about the meaning of its features, and to dwell upon the significant oddity of his having chosen to situate himself in Beverly Hills.

I had last been in Beverly Hills thirteen months ago— then, too, for *Life*—to interview Carl Sandburg, that monument who, upon the strength of a few early lines of genuine verse, had become an American literary success without ever becoming a poet. When I accepted the assignment I had only my schoolboy memory of his power. Rereading him, I was aghast at his thinness, and staggered by the difficulty of enclosing him (it was the assignment) in an article also about Robert Frost. After much discomfort I produced an article replete with matching images (Sandburg's affability, Frost's reluctance; Sandburg at 20th Century-Fox, Frost in a cabin in Vermont; Sandburg's name-dropping, Frost's confidence; Sandburg's grandiose quantification of all things, Frost's moral exactitude), sufficiently gaudy and enumerative to please Sandburg by its very acreage, sufficiently private and oblique to please Frost even more.

Mr. Nixon's house was not a luxurious house—wasn't the showplace the Democrats tried to make of it—and yet it wasn't the kind of house you or I would buy. It was, rather, a reception hall of the sort someone would buy whose requirement it was to assemble people not in intimacy but in mass, and whose activity of life was public, as

[36]

opposed to one whose discoveries occurred in silence or solitude.

Its interior, at entry, was of a solid, soft color tending toward white, immediately leading not farther inward but instantly outward, opening swiftly onto a patio. I had no sooner entered than I was out again, as if it were a trick house. I wondered how it was done.

Beyond the patio was a swimming pool. No story of Southern California is complete without a swimming pool. Mr. Nixon had one, the barking man of my story tried to commit suicide in one, and a swimming pool would appear significantly in the California Issue of *Life*. They were unavoidable, unless one were interested in the poor. As the crowd awaiting Mr. Nixon enlarged, its fringes approached the pool.

Not long before, one of the Kennedys, visiting California, had jumped (or fallen) into a swimming pool with his (or her) clothes on (I don't know the details), an incident Mr. Nixon referred to in his kickoff address the following morning, although his allusion failed to raise the partisan laughter he hoped for. He tried it twice again that day, tinkering with it, thinking it might be made to work, but although he varied his attack upon it he finally abandoned it, because he was prepared to abandon anything that didn't work. And it was that, in time—his absolute, hardheaded pragmatism—that helped me to see at last the perfect reasonableness of his having situated himself in Beverly Hills, where I had found Sandburg, where Marilyn Monroe lived and worked until she died, where life was always the public testing of workability. Politics was a career, like any other, all things urging Mr. Nixon forward within a system of values equally useful to a movie queen, as if politics were an entertainment, a show.

Could it be possible that a former Vice-President of the United States, twice almost President in a nuclear age, proceeds by the carnival values of Beverly Hills? To what sources, after this environment, would he turn in crisis? To the perspectives of history? Or to press agents? To the imagination of the outside possibility? Or to his public-opinion pollster?

Who were all these people? And where was Mr. Nixon? I had not yet seen him except in likeness in cartoons blown big on the wall of the alcove where drinks were mixed. The pattern of the cartoons was easy enough to trace, and extremely interesting: their central theme was Mr. Nixon's friendlessness, a comment upon his wide array of enemies, here reduced to a joke because, of course, it *had* to be a joke, because a man who had risen so high was bound to have *some* enemies—so there was *some* truth to it—but basically it couldn't be reality because it was caricature, enmity exaggerated, like the nose or the chin or the eyebrows of caricature.

It was an astute selection. Whose it was I didn't ask. It may have been his. Or at least he must have approved it, for the wall was his. I wondered if he knew what the pattern said. Later I became persuaded that he did not, that he had no idea what his wall meant; it was just there, and people got a kick out of it. The memory of his wall leaped to my mind many months later, after the election, when

[38]

Mr. Nixon was asked in a public place what he should be called, how addressed—Mr. Nixon or Dick or Mr. Former Vice-President or what—to which he replied, laughing, "Oh, I've been called everything," and laughing again, then, when his audience laughed, perhaps in relief because that was perhaps what had always hurt most, that long friendlessness amidst those familiar American particulars, the house, the esteem, the celebrity, the votes, the power. Marilyn Monroe died alone on a Saturday night, and nobody went to Gatsby's funeral.

I didn't know any of the people in the alcove, and they didn't know where Mr. Nixon was, or when he would arrive. They were campaign volunteers mainly, people who had helped him prepare for the present effort and who would help henceforth, who admired him, adored him, had a passion for him. They were well spoken, well dressed—some might have been financial contributors. To a gentleman smiling widely, though not at anyone in particular, I remarked upon the general *pattern* of the cartoons. He looked at them again, still smiling, and then at me, his smile never wavering, but his eyes filling with suspicion, then suddenly emptying. He had decided he had not heard me. He attributed his not hearing to the general hum of conversation behind us, accepting whatever it was I said as a well-intentioned but indistinct pleasantry, turning away, still smiling.

Somebody said, "He's here now," but it wasn't he; it wasn't anybody; and I drifted from the alcove to the newspapermen, many of whom I knew from the Governor's tour, and who introduced me to others—*Newsweek* was there, Los Angeles newspapers, San Francisco newspapers, somebody (I think) from the Knight chain, U.P.I., A.P., N.B.C., C.B.S. Nothing was likely to happen without its getting out. I asked who the people in the alcove were, but nobody seemed to know or care, and some of the newspapermen looked at me a little crossly, as if I shouldn't ask about things they considered irrelevant. I heightened my cordiality, received their opinions, and afterward drifted from here, too, back into the house, and stood again at the entry, making notes on the décor.

I had moved against the flow of guests, and I took the liberty, now, of wandering into the interior, which was deserted. I strolled shamelessly, to gain impressions by gathering symbols, and was immediately rewarded by my coming upon Mr. Nixon's library. Books were something I could make something of.

All were upon the shelves. There were many new books, recent books—books of travel, books of information, memoirs of prominent men in the news, and some novels (perhaps detective stories), but few I had heard of, and none I had read. The books offered the general impression of a practical man not given to symbolic routes toward illumination. There was no poetry there, and, to my surprise, no philosophy, though Mr. Nixon had mentioned in *Six Crises* the companionship of philosophy; no books of doubt or indirection. The works of Eisenhower were there, but not of Jefferson. It wasn't a library I'd want to be shipwrecked with; it carried no suggestion that the man who owned the house owned a vision of the end. Here were facts, maps, data, things you could verify without argument, so that your answer might be Yes or No or 21,365 but never Maybe or God Only Knows or, worst of all, I Don't Know. It was the library of a man training for a quiz show, and I knew now what he meant by "boning" and "homework," those words he had used with such regularity in *Six Crises,* numbers and names on the tip of your tongue, to give you the sound of decisiveness. Once, when Mr. Nixon was asked to comment upon the state of the arts in America, he produced figures showing the numbers of museums, theaters, symphony orchestras, *etc.,* percentage of increase in patronage, *etc.* He might easily have worked up those figures here in this library.

But if its dreariness depressed me, its honesty cheered me. Mr. Nixon could have chosen to stock his library with good books he wouldn't read, upon the advice of an informed person hired, like an interior decorator or a ghostwriter, to express acceptable emotions. It was better this way: better a short vision than deceit. For me, it was a discovery I was pleased to make, and to carry to the end: it was not that Mr. Nixon was deceitful; it was only that he knew no better: these were his limits.

Returning to the patio, I saw that he had still not arrived, but in the next moment, as I recall (though it might have been a full five minutes), I knew from the break of the voices that he had—the stir, the rippling, the crowd parting as it does when someone appears whom we have all been awaiting. I knew it from boyhood, from baseball stadiums, from the Polo Grounds especially, when a great star came down the clubhouse steps. I knew false alarms, cries of "Here he comes!" followed by the appearance of a dim star only, or a rookie, a nobody, when the stir and the rippling in the same instant rose and fell. But I knew when it was real, too, when it *was* Ott, *was* Terry, *was* Hubbell, or (at the World Series, 1936), *was* Gehrig, *was* DiMaggio, knew then to leap from my bleacher slab, marking my place in my book, to watch great men come, when the stirring and the rustling was its own excitement, as it was now, Mr. Nixon emerging from somewhere within the house, onto the patio, shaking hands.

He was not Ott, Terry, Hubbell, Gehrig, DiMaggio (his achievement would always be in doubt; theirs never), but he was a celebrity; his face and his voice and his name were known; therefore he ruled and unified the moment. He was the only man present whom everybody present knew, and therefore his importance was supreme, even for those who (not I), pretending to continue their conversations, kept him in the corners of their eyes, and even as he, a few minutes later, would catch me in the corners of his own, pretending to continue his conversation but flashing a question my way between eyelids narrowed and diverted for only a second, but in the question a dire caution; and I knew, former Vice-President or not, he was still a cat in the jungle subject at any moment to a fatal or crippling misstep. The place bristled with enemies, doubters, potential renegades, cynics, fair-weather friends, and newspapermen. He knew the names of some, and the faces. These faces he had located, and that was safe. But there were faces he did not know, and mine was one.

It was going to make a great deal of difference—to me, if not to him—how he reacted to my face, to me, to who I was, or what he thought I might be. I intended to begin by identifying myself as "of *Life*" (my reason for being here), and then, after a pause, as "a teacher up at San Francisco State College" (my qualification of my reason for being here, my further self announced), to see what his face would do with the second thought after whatever it did with the first. Under the first banner I might have been *for* him; under the second, probably not. I wanted to see by his face, if I could, whether he thought me capable of offering him equal treatment by a transcendence of my probable prejudice. If I could see what he thought my mind could do, I'd know something of his relationship to his own. Would he weigh me or count me—think of me as human or as type? Would he label me *egghead*, or *woolly-head*, and write me off, or did he understand, in spite of his library, that intellect imposed inquiry upon itself even at the cost of discovering itself in error?

(Now, of course, I shall be told how unfair I was. "Here is a man," you will say, "on the eve of a crucial campaign, with issues to be met, positions to be taken, a long trail ahead, reserves of energy to be found, resources to be tapped, hundreds of diverse and tricky problems to be solved—and you expect him to amuse himself by speculating upon *your* reality." Unfair, yes, or it would have been unfair had I not imposed the same conditions upon his adversary, pledging myself to begin to test him by his reaction to my slightly exceptional case, my failure to fit perfectly the familiar category, my being a reporter, but not quite, not fully earning my living that way, teaching school but not quite fully earning my living that way, either; I worked for the state but hadn't been appointed by the Governor, nor could he fire me for disrespect, so that the Governor himself was my superior only by virtue of my finding his character so. The Governor, too, the week before, caught me with his eye and threw out his hand and said, "I don't believe we've met." I thought it riskily said, because if he had met me he stood to lose me now for the crime of forgetting my name, and I couldn't help liking that—the risk he took, the flaunting of the old rule—standing and swaying in the aisle of the bus somewhere between Union Square and the airport on the night of the kickoff; I standing and swaying, he sitting, because there wasn't a seat near enough to him to suit my eavesdropping, trying not to like him, trying to harden my first sense of him, formed a few minutes before.

(From the platform at Union Square he had thrown his hat into the ring, an old gesture, an old tradition, poorly understood: a young man picked up the hat and handed it back. It was a bumbling, clownish moment, and I tried to fix him there, equalize him, this old-fashioned urban politician, tireless handshaker and backslapper, repository of names, custodian of appointments, sounding less like the governor of the nation's biggest state than like the fifth or the seventh politician on the platform, who would be permitted to say a few words to the local audience, have his photograph taken with top names on the ticket, but whom the smarter, the more advanced, the more liberal, the better-educated progressive young men of the party conspired to jettison as soon as the old guard had sufficiently died. His voice was high in his neck, his throat seeming to carry it all, piping it out. I waited for his lungs to supply resonance, but they didn't, as if some longtime appointee in charge of turning on the lungs had failed to report for work. The voice seemed at first too small a voice for so large a world: the billboards above us at Union Square advertised Qantas jets to the South Pacific, Lufthansa direct to Frankfurt, Pakistan International, B.O.A.C. "to all continents," and Richard M. Nixon—"Give California a Decisive Leader." The voice seemed at first too little deep, too little manly to do battle with Mr. Nixon. It was rasping, gravelly, lending itself to parody, and if, later, as it happened, you heard Mr. Nixon in his maleness challenging the Governor to "come out and fight like a man," to debate, man to man, voice to voice, you might have thought, Yes, one's a man and the other's not; I can tell by their voices.

(The Governor's hand was soft, puffy. Nobody had ever told him to cultivate a firm, strong handshake to create an image of robust manliness, or if anybody had he hadn't bothered. His voice and his hand and his handshake were his, something soft about him which he'd never tried to train away, seeming satisfied with, as if he was good enough for himself, you'd have to take him as he was.

(We flew to Salinas that night. On the airplane he told me—since I was a college professor—of his daughter's distress at the racial restrictions of college sororities. He said he believed the existence of such groups was a bad thing in state colleges. It was a perplexing problem—we had fought it out on our own campus—and I hated the idea of racial restrictions, but I believed the slow process of good education could kill it faster and better than Law. Burning to tell the Governor so, nevertheless I hesitated to quarrel with him less than an hour after meeting him. Debating with myself whether to quarrel, I was promptly freed by his asking me in his soft, indecisive way, "Don't *you* think so?")

Slowly, steadily Mr. Nixon advanced across the patio, shaking hands, chatting, and always moving, never really stopping, having in mind a private destination beyond this public place. He appeared rested, shaved, tan, lean, a firm man, not of a lounging disposition, hard, rigid, all sharp angles, all points at nose and chin: the cartoons on the wall of the alcove were less caricature than I had supposed. He advanced without visible haste, but his feet were impatient, and his body leaned in the direction of his intention, having somewhere to go. The Governor, under similar circum-stances, seldom appeared to have anywhere to go, having already arrived, pausing, talking, settling back upon his heels and characteristically inquiring, "How are things down here?" and remaining to absorb the answer, so that his aides were forever in the process of wrenching him away, herd-ing him to his bus so that the next engagement might be met, the schedule kept, time observed, duties done in a state so long and wide. Mr. Nixon, on the other hand, was self-propelling, both men, therefore, embodiments of what everyone told me they'd be: one soft, one hard; one loose, one tight; one open, one shut. Was I to find only what everyone had described in advance? What were the chances of my digging out a scoop for our regular weekly family magazine?

Now he was close. Perhaps he was five feet away. It was here that his eyes took me in, looked me over, washed round my face all in one second; and it was here, a moment later, when, according to an alternate plan, my little silver revolver somewhere up my sleeve was to have flashed forward with the motion of my hand, thrice fired, and I to cry, "*Sic semper tyrannis!*" fleeing back through the house, out the open door, down the hills, smiling at it now, offering him my hand, he smiling, too, returning my smile, I saying my name, naming my connections—*Life,* San Francisco State College—and adding upon impulse, "I already *have* a state job."

He delayed. He wanted to smile at the pleasantry, but he wanted a picture of the college first. Then he had it, then he smiled, then he said, "You need a bigger auditorium up there," quite surprising me, quite taking me aback, since, though we needed many things up there, one thing we didn't need was a bigger auditorium, as I burned to say, though I hesitated to quarrel with him so soon after meeting him. He did not ask, "What do *you* think?" Then he was gone.

He disappeared swiftly out of the public sector of the house into some private sector, perhaps to see his children, perhaps to make a telephone call, perhaps to meet with his speechwriters, or perhaps—as a newspaperman said—to shave. It was rumored that he was forever shaving, that he was pursued by the memory of the bad shave that had cost him (it was said) the first of the Kennedy television debates in 1960, after which (Mr. Nixon said in his own personal chapter in *Six Crises*) he won the others by better shaving; but the first was the biggest, its loss irrecoverable, and all for the want of a clean shave.*

Then he emerged. I couldn't tell if he had shaved: he looked neither more nor less shaved than before. Near the swimming pool he stepped up upon a pedestal of some sort —a stone, a box—welcoming the newspapermen to this newest campaign, to whom his Farewell Address at its end, two months later, would begin, "Good morning, gentlemen . . . and now that all the members of the press are delighted that I have lost, I'd like to make a statement of my own . . ." and conclude, "I leave you gentlemen now, and you will now write it. But as I leave you I want you to know—just think how much you're going to be missing. You won't have Nixon to kick around any more. . . ."

I think he thought the reason the newspapermen hated him (if indeed they did) was that they were liberals, union members—he thought it had something to do with their politics. But what they resented was his power, according to their apprehension of the uses of power. He was a mystery to them, his motives beyond their imagining. They thought he wanted the White House in the way they would have wanted the White House had the possibility existed

* Two and a half years later the loss of the Presidency (more readily verifiable than the winning or losing of TV debates) continued to plague him in the same terms. Asked how he would conduct the campaign if he had the chance again, he replied, "Well, I received so much advice after the election as to what I should have done that I am confident that if I had listened to all those people before, I would have lost by more than I did, so I really can't say. Maybe I should have used Bobby Kennedy as my makeup man. . . ."—quoted in the Boston *Globe*, April 21, 1963.

for them, because it was the very summit of influence, the metaphor of success, the best available job: therefore they ragged him in the same breath about the White House and about the Hughes Tool Company, from whom Mr. Nixon did or did not borrow money for his mother or his brother, or his mother for herself, saying, "I'm Richard's mother, you know," as if it were anything so uncomplicated as money Mr. Nixon was after, whose desire disdained money except as money bought relief from friendlessness.

Or they resented his virility, as they resent it in athletes. He could have had the girls if he wanted them, but he maddeningly didn't want them, and that was an insult to them who so much did but failed, their failure outcropping in self-betraying jokes telling of deprivation, slow action, poor relationships, emasculation, assuming in the listener his own poor functioning, and disbelieving that anyone at all really functions well.

They couldn't fix a scandal upon him, prove him vulnerable just like them, just like their readers, bringing him to earth as punishment for embarrassing them in the sight of their wives. The scandal might have been his bookshelves, but their own were not much different; the scandal might have been his limited vision, but theirs was hardly more expansive. The national scandal might be that relief from friendlessness may be sought in verification by vote, tabulated proof of one's being well liked, but this was an acceptable standard to men who, after all, measure their own success by circulation.

Officially he welcomed them—us—briefly, pleasantly, and, since he was about to present us with gifts, cautiously, stressing that these gifts were not from him but from the telephone company—flat, cheap briefcases of a kind of leather, not intended to last, our names engraved, containing handy data, memoranda, ball-point pens to swell my supply, pads, paper, a calendar (showing the academic year because, said Mr. Nixon, chuckling, "We are all eggheads"), and an itinerary of the tour we were about to make —a compact convenience quite like the one we had been given prior to our tour with the Governor, though on the Governor's tour the briefcases were simply handed to us without arduous explanation, the Governor never having been pressed, as Mr. Nixon was, to explain where his money came from, who assumed that we would assume it had been legitimately released from a fund legitimately accumulated: such an assumption Mr. Nixon could not make, for the men to whom he gave these gifts awaited a misstep and would have devoured him upon the very pads and paper with the very ball-point pens he had gifted them with, raised up a briefcase scandal whereby the little gifts could have become large gifts of expensive, lavish briefcases expensively and lavishly supplied with—as rumor grew—extravagant implements of every kind and cost, or even become enlarged, become altered, become something altogether different from briefcases, become deeds to properties, or loans in six figures.

Our gifts distributed, the party began to break. Before leaving, however, I went with Mrs. Nixon on a tour of the public sector of her house.

We were interrupted several times by departing guests coming out of their way to bid her good-bye, sometimes kissing her (the ladies, I mean), telling her how fine it had been, and how sweet she looked. It was as genuine as it could have been, however hard I looked for falsity in faces. She was a lady's lady. It was as genuine as, in turn, her own genuine disappointment at their departure. She was what she was, a whole person, and in being so was also in great measure one of the great strengths of her husband, attracting loyalty and faith to him by being herself so undoubted an example of devotion.

Observing her belief in him, I came to think she must have been instrumental in teaching him to believe in himself. Confident of his goodness, she possessed tangible objects, evidence sufficient to her mind, leading me here and there to show me the gifts of other admirers. Her enthusiasm was the private sensation of a lady whose house was hers, not the public act of the wife of a candidate. Nor was she compelled to explain the gifts, as her husband had explained the gifts to the newspapermen. She assumed that these gifts were an entitlement, earned by her husband's unassailable goodness: what could be more natural than expressions of affection toward Mr. Nixon?

I saw Oriental objects, gifts from far away, the very distance of their origin seeming, in her tone, to heighten their beauty. I touched them as we went, and she told me who sent each, and what each was—whatnots they were —never dreaming in her uncomplicated innocence that I might perceive in her whatnots the nature of their mistress, or trace the matter from the lady to her husband, or form in my mind the reasonable certainty that the line leading from one to the next might be the most reliable evidence I possessed of the quality of Mr. Nixon's vision or belief: for nothing here was esthetically useful. It wasn't what you or I would have exhibited.

Not the alleged loans of money nor the alleged presidential ambition, but those books and these whatnots were the scandal. I felt, with Henry Adams, viewing Ulysses S. Grant, witness to the disproof of Darwinian theory.

Thus ended my tour of her white house. Then, alone, I drifted again to Mr. Nixon's library. The meaning of his books having begun to weigh upon me, my intention was to copy their titles on my California Legal, and afterward to study their pattern at my leisure. But I had scarcely begun my task when Mr. Nixon entered in the company of two assistants, all of whom, seeing me there, abruptly suspended their conversation. There was a small distress in Mr. Nixon's eyes: requiring my departure, he hated to be rude. I might have said, "For my article, you see, it will help me to understand you, so please give me an hour to copy down the titles of your books," except that it would have sounded, to him, quite mad. What had a man's reading to do with his capacity to govern? Therefore I didn't say it, but simply left, going back through the house, which was quiet now, as after a party, or—to be more pointedly analogous—as after a last rehearsal before a first performance. Tomorrow Mr. Nixon would open; his kickoff. It would be the beginning of his new beginning, or the beginning of his end.

I was driven back to the Biltmore by a Nixon volunteer, a college student of whose name I made no note, and whom

I never saw again. He was blond, handsome, wealthy. His father was a friend of Mr. Nixon of long standing, and the boy was therefore, or by conviction, or both, strong for Mr. Nixon, as I had been, twenty-two years before, because of my father and because of my conviction, strong for Mr. Willkie.

He drove me through the Strip, saying there were girls here. I knew there were girls there. I could see the bright lights. But he had no way of knowing what I knew, as I had not known, twenty-two years before, what old men of thirty-nine knew.

He was a good boy, studying law somewhere, wanting the right things to happen, and looking for the rules that made things go. We took a hurried supper at a crowded restaurant near the Biltmore, where he was mildly dismayed to see that people who had arrived later than we were served before we were, that the rightness and order of things were awry. This small outrage was consistent with suspicions he had apparently been gathering at college, and which were beginning to undermine him by placing all verities in question, beginning with his father and ending with the study of law. He asked me what I thought of his going in for the law—wasn't it a right thing to do? I told him to teach law for a living, trying cases only as a sideline—not to mix winning at law with the *art* of law. Perhaps I was wrong. I was thinking of writing, not of law, and of politics, too, and of Mr. Nixon in particular, whose life now hung upon his winning; who, if he lost, would have no other, would for a while beat and thrash in the councils of his party, issuing statements, issuing opinions, gradually declining.

He asked me what I thought of Mr. Nixon. Damn if I knew, I more or less said. Damn if I knew about the law, either. "For God's sake," I said, "don't listen to anything I say." If I hadn't *seen* Mr. Nixon it'd be easy enough to have an opinion. That's the trouble (I said) with evidence; it confuses me. There were too many facts, too many issues, too much space; it was all a guess, all a matter of discovering a method of perception, sizing up the whatnots, grasping the symbols flying off everything.

And yet—not to be too modest about it—I had recently a surge of confidence in my guessing. Many things had seemed to turn out as I had said they would, though I had never possessed what people call evidence. I knew that the girls were where the lights were.

In my room in the Biltmore I wrote in my Journal (private pages quite apart from my California Legal): "I don't know what to think of Nixon. He doesn't seem to be a villain—but how can I tell?" The words were a triumph, a fight I had won. I had hoped to reserve judgment, and I seemed to have done so, to have subdued my prejudices, kept my mind open.

Undressing, I knew that I had not sweated. Had I been hostile I would have been nervous, and had I been nervous I would have sweated, but I had not sweated. No sweat. Nor had I smoked cigarettes. Had I sweated I would have smoked cigarettes. My mind was clean; I was in shape, the rubble of my past cleared away. I had not shot him, but cordially shaken his hand, cordially chatted, and been a gentleman to his wife. I sat resting, smoking a slow cigar by my window at the Biltmore, admiring myself in the mirror of my reminiscence, thinking how grandly civilized I'd become, what heights of dispassion I'd scaled.

But in bed, reviewing things, backing up, ruminating, I began to ponder his pleasantry: What did he mean to say when he said we needed a bigger auditorium? We didn't need a bigger auditorium. What we needed, if anything, was a smaller one. No doubt he meant to say—not to be too immodest about it—that when he had spoken in our auditorium he had filled it, overspilled it.

But, my dear man, I argued, the purpose of our auditorium is to accommodate lecture and drama, not to accommodate occasional former Vice-Presidents, of whom we haven't many, after all, and who visit us only in election seasons. Our auditorium . . .

The matter could not have occupied me for long. I remember beginning to rise, having forgotten to lower the window shade, but falling back again and sleeping hard in utmost serenity, and waking fresh and early, the shade still up.

CHAPTER 3 ☞

For weeks afterward—after **Mr.**
Nixon and the Governor had seen the last of me, after my
article was written, and after I was securely back in my
classroom teaching American Values—the bookmark in my
Emerson was the memorandum handed to me at Nixon
headquarters on Wilshire Boulevard: "Nixon bus will leave
8:00 a.m. Wednesday from the Grand Street entrance of
the Biltmore Hotel."

Mr. Nixon was not on it. It was the press bus, and everybody was fresh and alert and high-spirited, or so it seemed
to me who was, after my serene night. We wore plastic
lapel badges reading WIN WITH NIXON, carrying his mes-

sage docilely, as one captively carries the dealer's message on a new car, more or less amiably resenting it, more or less bereft of the will to remove it. On the Governor's tour it hadn't been done quite this way: our badges identified us, but they didn't say WIN WITH BROWN, affording us access without demanding commitment. It was a small point, but not without meaning, and I thought the contrast worth a line on my California Legal.

Somebody gave me a copy of the speech Mr. Nixon would deliver at Pomona, but I didn't want it, and I waved it away with a magniloquent gesture more impressive to myself than to anyone else. But a large point of principle was at stake: I didn't want to be a party to the binding of Mr. Nixon to his text. I wanted him to break from it, and free himself, if that was what he wanted for himself. I wanted to hear what he said between and beyond the lines of his promissory text, and I didn't want to copy anything down that I hadn't heard for myself.

(Word had got round, I know, that I was queer and cranky. The Governor, one night, at a place called Los Banos, had thought to abandon his prepared address and talk off the cuff. It was a charming idea, a charming address. We had driven into Los Banos past dry plains which the Governor's Water Plan would irrigate, and he felt powerful about that, as if he himself would bear the water on his own shoulders, priest, god, magician, creating life where none had been, the band at Los Banos greeting him with "Stairway to the Stars," the minister referring in his benediction to "the Supreme Governor," meaning God, and a wild surplus of barbecued steaks cooked by the chief of police.

"I like campaigning," the Governor said, beginning his speech, "because I like people," though he wished, he frankly said, there were fewer people and more intimacy; sometimes he envied those governors of small states a man can walk around. Frankly, he said, he'd be spending most of his time in Southern California where the people were not necessarily better but were positively more numerous—still warming up to his speech, or so I thought. "I could make a speech as long as Fidel Castro," said the Governor, announcing—someone passed up a memorandum—the baseball score, and remarking that the Governor's mansion was built the same year his mother was born, though she was in better repair now than the mansion was, and presenting Bill Flynn of *Newsweek*, who had collaborated on an article about California.

(The Governor's discursiveness prevented his ever arriving at the prepared speech distributed beforehand to the newspapermen and even now set in type in distant cities to be read in the morning as the true and accurate record of what had occurred last night at Los Banos. I remember Carl Greenberg of the Los Angeles *Times* leaning against a wall, killing his story by telephone, disconsolate, and I argued with him into the night that he ought to have reported what was said, not merely killed what wasn't, especially since, in the present speech, what was said was instructive, lively, expressing the character of the Governor. Greenberg seemed to be saying it was the Governor's responsibility to honor the prepared address, that somehow the event was less important than the report in the press. I argued . . . but why argue? He was a steady man, a veteran of dependable habits, he who was afterward, in Mr. Nixon's Farewell Address, specifically exonerated from the general charge of bias, an old pro riding the buses and eating the steaks and filing the handouts. My mind fled to Port Chester, New York, and the old pro on the *Daily Item*, whose overshoes I inherited: "When you've done it as long as me, you won't do it any better.")

Then we were at the fairgrounds at Pomona, where I wanted to hear what came out of Mr. Nixon, not what came off pages prepared beforehand. It was a cool, gray morning, the leaves were turning, the cheerleaders were cartwheeling, and the band was playing "On Wisconsin," somewhat irrelevantly, I thought, for I knew of no Nixon connection to Wisconsin. A minister prayed, "God keep us from the littleness of little men." Prayer, anthem, Pledge of Allegiance—there were always these rituals to remind us of our intentions, of the ideals we began with or liked to think, afterward, we had begun with.

My plastic badge crying WIN WITH NIXON carried me easily through the crowd. I had thought it well, on the Governor's tour, not so much to face the speaker as to face the crowd, to watch the people watching. I did so now, trying to make something of the people. Sid Kossen, of the San Francisco *Examiner*, said, "The place is crawling with Birchers," but I couldn't follow his logic. This crowd, I suspected, had come to the support of Mr. Nixon from directions as diverse as we who had been for Mr. Willkie at the Empire Race Track. A speaker said from the stage, "It's a question of trying to time yourself with a helicopter," listening into the air for the sound of Mr. Nixon's helicopter, and adding somewhat woodenly, to fill the empty moment, "The eyes of the nation are on Pomona today." He was the nervous local chairman whose hour had arrived, but whose star hadn't.

In this district Mr. Nixon's political life had begun. From here he had gone to Congress. Here he had begun his campaign for the Presidency in 1960. Here Mr. Nixon's policy, party, and style had been decreed, ordained, forcing upon him that side of the debate he had always taken, and to which he was committed. He had risen and fallen. Now he would try going upward again.

In a practical way, Mr. Nixon took hope from the fact that he had never lost California: in the weeks ahead he would often mention that reality. But the year was different now. It was no longer the fearful year of McCarthy, 1952; no longer were there Eisenhower coattails to fly upon, as in 1956; his opponent now was not the untried Kennedy of 1960 but the Governor, whose four-year stewardship had been thorough and clean. Thus Mr. Nixon was alone now in a way he had never been alone before.

Perhaps he knew his chance was bad. Perhaps not. Either way, he might have begun to run now in the knowledge of loss, as all brave runners run, inspiring us by running hard, even as schoolboys run, racing on, though they know from the outset they cannot win, running with a miracle in mind. Mr. Nixon might have said to himself, with history in mind, "Lose now, win later."

On the other hand, career in America seldom permits a turning back from the style, the policy, the specialty, and the commitment of first fame, no change of mind or heart, no growth, and Mr. Nixon had situated in Beverly Hills, where career was all.

Then we heard his helicopter, which had lost its way, and then he came, his arm about his wife, into this innocence, this faith, for these people at Pomona, like the people who had eaten barbecued steak with the Governor at Los Banos, caring little for the practical politics of the prepared address, cared infinitely more for the reality of Mr. Nixon than for his newspaper image. They were ready to accept any departure he might make, and to follow.

This was impressed upon me by a stunning, unplanned act. I had been wandering through the crowd, but I had begun to saunter to the press tables when the official course of things was diverted by an involuntary chant, rising and spreading and at last unanimously adopted, "Down in front . . . down in front . . . down in front." Like all mob action, it chilled the blood.

Its object was the massed cameras and photographers on an elevated platform obscuring the crowd's view of Mr. Nixon, who, onstage, arms upraised, was smiling, to show that he knew the hostility was directed somewhere other than at him, though of its object he might have been uncertain, the crowd crying now with heightened determination, "Down in front . . . down in front . . . down in front," not merely rhythmically but murderously, and I thought afterward of the soldiers and peasants of Faulkner's *A Fable* who, with peace and armistice within their power, hadn't known it, who in the fury of their innocence could have ended the war had they understood their power, as the people of Pomona could have won a significant victory by sustaining their chant.

The photographers, huddled beside their cameras on the exposed platform, would willingly have retreated, eagerly fled, surrendered Mr. Nixon to the people of Pomona, whom he might then have addressed out of the discoveries of his best private heart. His will was their desire. He was a hero returned from afar, local boy made good, Dick The Grocery Boy returned from the threshold of the White House. He was at liberty to speak daringly. Now I, too, from the midst of this crowd, my breast emblazoned WIN WITH NIXON, joyously added my voice to the chant, chanting, "Down in front . . . down in front . . . down in . . ." until at last my throat refused to exert itself beyond its safe limit, as at the Empire Race Track in my boyhood.

It would have been a victory for us all had Mr. Nixon then and there urged the removal of the cameras, addressing only the human faces before him, as if they and they alone were the horizon of his desire, as if he didn't care for his picture in the newspapers. But he made no such decision. Order returned. The photographers rose and reassumed their stations—though when, soon afterward, a flashbulb smackingly exploded, they recoiled as a body, winced, and tucked in again, all jitters still. I worked my way back to the press tables. "Place crawling with Birchers," I said.

Mr. Nixon had been presented to the crowd as "the greatest Vice-President in the history of the country," a complimentary advertisement he reciprocated by praising

[63]

"the best fair in the United States," though it hadn't opened yet. Perhaps he meant the best fair year-in year-out, an interpretation my editor at *Life* later urged upon me, and which I sourly accepted during one of several last-minute editorial consultations, when *Life* was trimming away vestiges of my hysterical prejudice beyond those I had trimmed away myself.

The crowd cheered. He spoke again, he was cheered again; several times perhaps; I didn't count. These were prepared remarks, old stuff, stretches of sound track, nothing everybody hadn't heard before, and the cheering was becoming a bit perfunctory when he delivered a fine sentence which gave me hope. I thought he was going to break a little loose now.

"We have got to have a reason to be against those we are against," said Mr. Nixon.

It had rhythm, that sentence. I hear it now, in Mr. Nixon's voice, coming up out of him. Feeling its rhythm, I closed my eyes and halted my thoughts, going back over the rhythm that would give me the language verbatim and writing it on my California Legal. I knew it couldn't possibly have appeared in the prepared text.

It was his thinking out loud, his literary criticism of his speech thus far, an accurate explanation of the diminishing applause. He had gone plunging into himself for vitality. It was his discovery, that phenomenon I had tried to describe to Alvin Moscow at lunch.

Yet this good sentence earned him no applause, though he must have expected it, since he paused then as if he did, unless he was only listening to it himself, admiring it, as a writer might pause to admire a well-wrought line, or as a baseball player might pause, stand, his bat draped across his shoulder, admiring the flight of a long foul ball. It was a silence we all know, when our good effect has been lacking in preparation, when our main lines of attack have failed, and we sense before our audience itself has sensed it that this is not to be our day.

Perhaps he was stale after long inaction. Moreover, his throat was giving him difficulty. In any case, he returned to his prepared remarks:

Capital punishment. He favored it (the Governor opposed it). *not too much applause,* I wrote on my California Legal.

He not only favored capital punishment but favored its extension to include a vague category of persons he called "big-time dope peddlers."

But that didn't draw much applause, either.

Therefore he once again abandoned his prepared remarks and went back to himself, seizing precisely that image a free-flowing mind, on a morning going poorly, might well have gambled on—the delay of his helicopter, the confusion he had seen from that air, the blighted and altered landscape, the encroachments of steel upon the countryside of his boyhood, "the oranges, the lemons, and the avocados gone," he said, when again the rhythm captured me, and captured him, too, and evoked a sputtering of applause, not for the blight and encroachment but as an encouragement to him to amplify. Thereupon he punctured it, ended it, and returned to his prepared address, lest this discovery of a new direction lure him into implications he dared not pursue: a

[65]

public affection for Nature at the expense of factories and missile sites would not have been a winning issue in 1962, and he had gathered upon his shelves no books in praise of loss.

His voice strengthened. The health of his throat was a barometer of his confidence. By evening his throat would be strong and clear, his energy up. His stamina was remarkable to begin with, and he was good at recuperation. He said he worked best at the edge of weariness.

The kickoff at Pomona ended with the band's playing "Anchors Aweigh." There was a relevance to it, since Mr. Nixon had been in the Navy in a way he had never been in Wisconsin. I heard it as our bus began to move, and I wrote it down, *band playing anchors aweigh*, and, to catch my mood, *things bound to go bad now*. I meant for me. I didn't know about him. But I began to suspect, by the irregular confidence of his voice, that his strength for the campaign would come only from the sound of himself when it sounded most as he'd sounded in the past. If he had had any plans to break from his past, Pomona discouraged them. There would be no New Nixon, and I was beginning to feel the faintest blue.

Luckily, just at this moment, I encountered Steve Hess. He was at the back of the bus, and he must have been reading down the roster of the press party because when he came forward he had the roster in his hand, looking for me, asking for me behind me in such a voice that I knew who he was: he was a reader, though what kind of reader I had no way of knowing—one of those rare good readers, I hoped, who asked the questions I wanted to be asked. But there was always that lousy first one—"Are you *the* Mark Harris?" he asked.

"That's such a damn embarrassing question," I said.

He sat beside me. He was a good reader, it proved. I wouldn't have expected to find him writing speeches for Mr. Nixon (I would have expected to find him teaching Politics at a university), but he had somehow, in the course of academic study, encountered a Republican senator, and in the course of this encounter encountered President Eisenhower, for whom, I believe, he wrote some speeches, and who then lent him or gave him or sent him to Mr. Nixon. He was a short, energetic fellow, a bit harried, his arms always full of papers and documents, but he was blessed with the capacity, at a moment's notice, to burrow among them, find what he needed, and set to work on almost any horizontal surface.

I told him I had begun to feel blue about Mr. Nixon, that I had hoped to discover a man with a vision of the end, but that I had been disappointed; that I had hoped to find a New Nixon, but that I didn't think he had any plans along that line; that I had begun by trying to view the Governor and Mr. Nixon as equally meritorious, leaning, even, a little toward Mr. Nixon, but that both were making things hard for me.

Hess was astonished. His reading of my books had persuaded him of my general intelligence, but his hearing me speak so stupidly now quite puzzled his expectations. In vigorous, persuasive language, with ample reference to scholarly books and reliable sources, he showed me how, by welding together disparate elements of the California

Republicans, and by lending his person to the cause, Mr. Nixon was offering the strongest possible bulwark against the worst tendencies of entrenched power.

Did I want one-party politics in California? Certainly not. Hess forced me to reevaluate some of my supposed evidence, to hold up my images against a slightly different light, and so see other dimensions of things. It was a relief to do so, and to hear from Hess, in subsequent conversations, of anecdotes and incidents appealing not only to my political sense but also to my symbolic sense—moments Hess could recall, and poetically present, when Mr. Nixon was guided by humane considerations at the expense of politics, moments of kindness and tenderness proving warmth and compassion never sufficiently conveyed to those of us who knew Mr. Nixon only through television or other inadequate media. Like others of Mr. Nixon's staff, Hess had joined in skepticism and grown to passion.

My relationship to Hess reminded me of an incident. We have a friend—my wife and I—who was once brutally and disgustingly raped by a Negro who had gained admission to her apartment, as he had to others, by posing as a crippled stamp collector, crutches, album, and all. She was a girl whose triumph of life had been, after hard internal struggle not simplified by her upbringing in a scatterbrained family, her conviction of the brotherhood of men, not excluding Negroes. After her misfortune she regularly visited—as if he were a doctor—a friend whose role it became to persuade her anew of all she had so laboriously taught herself. I was like her now. My mind, though only recently open, was in danger of closing. More than once I would hurry to Steve Hess.

On the flight to San Diego I was feeling better, almost serene, as I had been the night before. I wanted to talk more to Hess, but we had become separated. There were two airplanes, one for Mr. and Mrs. Nixon, their staff, and reporters chosen by lot, but I had not won this leg of the journey in the drawing and was therefore on the other airplane—the wrong airplane—alone with my notes, my reflections, and my revival of spirit.

Mr. Nixon was to speak at San Diego upon the subject of education. If I did not fully understand the water problem, or crime or welfare or taxes or agriculture or other issues many people seemed to understand, I knew something of education. I thought I could make a clear judgment there.

The Governor's views upon the subject had never entirely satisfied me. He had a solid instinct for it—one saw in his son the freedom the father had granted, for clearly his son had been asked a thousand times, "What do *you* think?" But the Governor's public review of his program in education fell short of winning me. He praised a Master Plan whose very name revolted me; he had counted campuses and buildings, and promised more, as if *more* meant *better;* and he placed too great faith in an enormous testing program, seeming to assume that by measuring what we had we'd automatically improve it.

We were late to San Diego—to the Palm Room of the U. S. Grant Hotel, steaming with the heat of a crowd twice as large as comfort required. Somebody said there were twelve hundred people, and I wrote it down. Many of the people were finishing their lunches, though others had scarcely begun, and as I struggled to the front of the room I had at least the opportunity to review, course by course, a meal I was not destined to eat. Finding no place at table for myself, I sat on the apron of the stage, where I was not served but could help myself from trays on carts parked near me, picking at a lunch too unnatural to appease me— now a bit of ice cream, now a celery stalk, now an unbroken hard roll. It seemed a small sacrifice I was obliged to make, to hear Mr. Nixon direct, rather than to have gone to the press room, where I could have received both a balanced lunch and a copy of his prepared address.

Mr. and Mrs. Nixon, though a way was cleared for them through the dense room, experienced much difficulty in reaching the speakers' tables. They must have rejoiced at the size and evident excitement of this crowd (the Governor a week before had drawn very poorly in the same room), which was partly Republican and partly invited Democratic guests, people "not committed" to Mr. Nixon, one speaker said, but "with minds open"—like my own, or as I was trying to keep it, anyhow.

Mr. Nixon, after preliminary speakers, and after his own preliminary remarks—he praised the San Diego "team," pledged to serve four years as governor, once again tried out the humorous sequence involving the Kennedy in the swimming pool, reissued his challenge to the Governor to debate face-to-face on television, and urged all of us whose minds were still open to "listen to us, ask us questions"—slowly approached the question of education. I was eager and hopeful. This was my job he would be talking about, a definition of my role as teacher and what it ought to entail.

Then he began with a question—a good procedure in teaching. "What are our schools for," he asked, "if not for indoctrination against Communism?"

The idea shocked me, and I saw, too, a tremor pass through the crowd. I was facing the crowd, as Mr. Nixon was, and he must have seen what I saw, a stiffening, a sudden upturning of heads and straightening of backs, for he began to qualify what he had said, reducing the breadth of his remark, having said too much and gone too far, bid too high and so begun to bargain now. But he had lost with a single breath the best open attention of a considerable body of people who had come to see if he was new or old, and who knew of education, whatever else they might or might not have known, that it could never be so simply *that*.

The moment had been so poorly chosen for a sentence so dogmatic that I began to wonder, as I would often wonder afterward, whether it was not his hidden will to lose, his wish, concealed even from his own eye, to end himself in politics and thereby end the tension between himself and what he had once begun, to free himself for some better life. I remember, soon after, in a factory where he had been shaking hands, his coming suddenly, abruptly—his almost shattering his face—against a steel pillar bearing a 1960 banner leering KENNEDY, then turning to see if I had seen, and smiling, rueful, chagrined, bedeviled by chance beyond

[71]

his control, his smile seeming to say that someday there'd be an end to it, and not unwelcome. I liked him immensely then.

But I didn't like him now. I didn't like what he had said. I didn't like his revising the whole idea of teaching. We had been through all that in California, suffered it, and although we still signed "loyalty" oaths they had become a formality. It was a debate we were unlikely to resume. We had settled the question of "indoctrination" in free exchange, even as we had decided for ourselves with our own intelligence upon the proper size of our auditorium.

I had had enough for the moment. I passed from the room, looking for Steve Hess but not seeing him. I looked for him in the press room, but he wasn't there, either. He wasn't anywhere, and just when I needed him.

From the lobby of the U. S. Grant I telephoned my old friend Jean Tozer. A decade before, we had been neighbors, living with our beginning families in little metal war-surplus huts near the University of Minnesota. Her husband and I were nearing the end of the long student trail.

Our field was American Civilization. Some scholars in traditional studies denied the existence of a civilization under that name, but we who explored it came to believe in its formidability, seldom with more direct usefulness than I in this moment, knowing she was there. Her voice pacified my rising hysteria, recalling with special appropriateness the long discussions we had had about Senator McCarthy, who had also believed in "indoctrination," but whom American civilization, loyal to broader forms of education, ground through its process, censured, and discharged at last.

The senator immediately died, and I wondered why I had ever feared him.

And why, now, should I fear again? Mr. Nixon, too, was an aspect of American civilization. His kind had always grown in the garden, always briefly flourished, and always early died. History was abundant with his variety, and one feared him only if one were ignorant of history. What was my education for, if not to sustain me now?

Where was I?—she was asking—what doing and for how long?

"I'm with the Nixon campaign," I said.

"Oh, Mark," she said, in a falling inflection.

Quickly I explained. "The big problem," I said, "is getting off at a distance from my emotions, putting him in the context of history. I don't think he has too thrilling a vision of the end."

"I knew that," she said.

"I've got to write about it," I said; "I can't just say I knew it. Whatever he is, good or bad, I've got to assume he believes it. I've got to find a tone, you know what I mean? A viewpoint." She listened. She knew I was in some sort of trouble I was working out for myself. (She had been a psychiatric nurse at the University of Minnesota, specializing in disturbed children.) "What I'm after is as much absolute objectivity as I can muster up. I'm going to be beautifully detached. It'll be like I was writing about some old election nobody cares anything about any more, like Bryan and McKinley, something along those lines. Here's a good sentence I invented on the airplane just before: 'All hysteria arises from a deficiency of historical perspective.' "

"I'm voting for the Governor," she said.

I saw him next at the airport. It was my turn to fly with him now, our first time up together and a difficult moment for me since, though I was enraged at him, it was impractical for me to hope his plane could crash. *Lv San Diego Convair 240*, says my California Legal, but there must have been a brief delay because I changed *240* to *250*.

He sat at the front of the—what do you call it?—that commodious cabin of private airplanes, where one can work, nap, drink, smoke, talk, think, on a deep swiveling chair. He could have turned to talk to me if he wished, though he didn't, having work to do and energy to conserve. In any case I had already asked all the small questions I could think of—did he smoke? did he drink? was he relaxed about airplanes? how often did he telephone his children?—as a way of beginning. He lingered so long in reply I never posed the larger, which may have been what he preferred. No matter, he was answering them all without my asking.

His wife sat on a similar chair across the aisle from him, the two leading, so to speak, a parade of chairs double-file through the air. Up ahead, their door open, sat two pilots who were not, I hoped, as enraged as I by Mr. Nixon's views on education. It was not out of the question, or anyhow not beyond my imagination, that in my rage I might at any moment go berserk, rushing forward to the place of the pilots and leaping upon them and flailing about among the controls until, striking the right (or the wrong) buttons and levers I should send the whole craft plunging down among the mountains or valleys of California, thus ending my career and his, and the careers of the pilots and newspapermen. My *Sic semper tyrannis* would rattle its final echo in the wilderness, and the newspapers would be filled with bipartisan expressions of regret, along with demands for an investigation into a mishap so inexplicable.

Only the back of Mr. Nixon's head was visible to me. His legs were outstretched, his feet resting in the magazine rack. He was outlining, revising (eavesdropper, I am also peeper), preparing a speech more acceptable to himself than the two he had thus far made; still trying out; still on the road (the metaphor of theater was forming in my mind); still searching for the right mixture of things, for that sufficiently forceful but sufficiently ambiguous message which would be Left enough to please his Left without displeasing his Right, and Right enough to please his Right without displeasing his Left.

So it was possible for me, understanding this, to modulate my emotions, and even, by thinking along lines suggested by Steve Hess, to sympathize with Mr. Nixon's task.

I was steadier now. To show myself how steady I was I walked forward and stood behind the pilots who so coolly guided this machine into an unknown known only to them. I liked to think my job would appear as complex to them as theirs appeared to me. Casually I lit a cigarette and casually turned, discovering that Mrs. Nixon had been staring at the back of my head not less earnestly than I, a few moments before, had been staring at the back of her husband's. Did she know, by familiar signs or clues, that I was a type who normally hated her husband and would cast

[75]

him out of his job, just as he (if by *teaching* we mean *indoctrination*) would cast me out of my own because, by his standard, I was unfit? She smiled and said, speaking of the luncheon at the U. S. Grant Hotel, "Wasn't it exciting!"

She was to say it twice again on other occasions—"Wasn't it exciting!" I thought at first it was a gambit to engage my enthusiasm, but I finally came to believe her too genuine for gambits. Things *were* exciting to her. She sought and always found the happy and encouraging complexion to events, life having gone, on the whole, so well for her. She had amazingly risen in her lifetime "from Nowhere up to Somewhere," in Frost's phrase—from nothing up to something, nobody up to somebody. Beginning as Pat The Typewriter Girl, becoming wife of the Vice-President, she had produced her sequel to Dick The Grocery Boy or Mark The Glove Boy in that inexhaustible series of books made in America by Horatio Alger. "Or maybe," she added, seeing that I did not share her excitement, "you don't agree." She wore a white orchid sprinkled with stardust.

"I didn't agree with *everything* he said," I said, asking abruptly, thinking of my metaphor of theater, "I saw in some biographical material about you that you and Mr. Nixon once played together in a play. . . ."

She smiled, remembering. "In *The Dark Tower*," she said.

It had a perfect sound, and I wrote it into my California Legal. They played, she told me, the romantic leads, and I wondered how it would be to be her director. "I suppose," I said, "these tours get pretty boring."

[76]

"No," she said, "every day is different."

I would cast her as a girl younger than she was, for whom every day was different, one who was disinclined to organize the items of the spectacle, seeking no central principle of life, and unaware that there might be a principle to discover, even as she was unaware of the absolute, principled coherence of her whatnots. I yearned to direct her. As teacher, I yearned to teach her, to possess her Socratically in my classroom. (On one occasion we talked about opportunity in America. I argued that opportunity was frequently denied to many people. I was thinking of Negroes. Perhaps I said so. "But look at Dick and I," she said, not looking quite at me. Many people were poor, I said; many people began in bad health; all was far from equal even in this good place. "But look at Dick and I," she said again, almost looking at me now.) In time I could have reached her. I would have given much for one divine semester with her.

For the moment, however, I passed on, back to my seat, observing soon thereafter that she had taken off her shoes and fallen asleep. Her husband, across the aisle, was likewise asleep, or appeared to be. Of her I was certain, of him not. He may have been only thinking. His papers were on his lap, his pencil lay between his fingers, and his attitude was sleep, though it may have been only rest: it was not the day for sleep; the fight was on, and he had always fought hard, tirelessly, ceaselessly, proud of what a college friend once called his "iron butt," that capacity to work beyond fatigue.

As for me, recovering my poise, I turned my attention to plans for my article.

[77]

It was here, on the fortieth page of my California Legal, that I began a skeletal holding framework, experimenting with a projection of my tone, my focus, beyond the present, into some historical future. Posing as remote historian, I could relieve myself of my emotional attachment to events surrounding the California gubernatorial election of 1962. As historian, I needn't care. My blood needn't boil. If, as writer, my role were well acted I would become so immersed in my pretense that even in the act of writing I would at some point be startled to lift my eyes and discover (for it would be October then) the 1962 campaign still in progress, the winner still undetermined, the candidates still living. *Impossible*, I would think. (Indeed, something of the sort did occur. One afternoon, the writing almost done, I broke for an hour to take my son to his cello lesson at a studio near the corner of Divisadero and California streets, in San Francisco. Cello in hand, I was crossing that intersection when a Trailways bus, bedecked with a banner, WIN WITH NIXON, hissed to a stop at the traffic light. I saw familiar shapes, the Nixons, their aides, newspapermen, all quite as I had left them, still sitting there, still riding around and around and around, condemned to that particular eternity. Nobody looked out at me, and to a great extent, because of the tinted windows, I could not distinctly see in. I called, I waved, I held my son's cello aloft to attract attention, but behind the greenish panes not a head turned. All within were immobile, dead, ghosts, except for the driver, who, when the light changed, lifted his elbow from the steering wheel, where it had been resting, whereupon the bus glided forward and was gone.)

[78]

My tone imagined, I needed a point to begin, and I thought I knew just where. The historian Frederick Jackson Turner, of the University of Wisconsin (could that be why the band was playing "On Wisconsin" at Pomona?), had called attention in 1893 to an event which had occurred unnoticed —the United States census report of 1890 declaring the end of the American frontier. "This brief official statement," Turner wrote, "marks the closing of a great historic movement. Up to our own day American history has been in a large degree the history of the colonization of the Great West. The existence of an area of free land, its continuous recession, and the advance of American civilization westward, explain American development."

Turner read the symbols flying off history. I had first heard of the Turner thesis at the University of Minnesota; I had since used it as a document in my classroom; and it had been suggestive to my thinking in at least two of my works of fiction. At a simple level, the westward movement, first from Europe to the Atlantic seaboard, and then by stages to California, was inspired by two principal emotions. One I could call Economic, and say it was represented by the Governor. The other I could call Individualistic, and say it was represented by Mr. Nixon. *Bread and butter Brown* vs. *individualistic Nixon* I wrote on my California Legal. I could play with it.

My notes also show the phrase *the historian would*, followed by the question to myself, *Can I carry a whole article in the future indefinite tense?* I thought I could (without knowing if such a tense existed); I thought I *had* to. It was essential for me to force my language to serve some objective end distant from my own potential hysteria, or prejudice or passion or whatever it was.

Time and space did wonders for my disposition. By the time we completed the flight from San Diego to Sacramento my spirits had risen, and I had in hand a serviceable outline:

I. Quote Turner thesis as much as possible, just typing it out is enriching.

II. California now 112 years old.

III. Nov. 6 election, would it be Nixon or Brown. Calif biggest state now, quite a jump from 1890 census to 1970. Westward movement now complete for the second time. New new west. Turner found his meaning. What's the new new meaning?

IV. Nov. 6 election, would it be Nixon or Brown. How they campaigned: Playwright Nixon vs. Lawyer Brown.

V. What they represented. Bread and butter Brown vs. individualistic Nixon. Urban Brown vs. Rural Nixon. Take one and then the other like with Sandburg and Frost, matching image for image, Collectivist Brown vs. free enterprise nixon, mercy brown vs. gas chamber nixon, Welfare brown vs economy nixon etc etc federal brown vs. local nixon, san francisco brown vs. pomona nixon.

VI. What the historian could not know. Future indefinite tense. Be objective, but in the end have a little opinion in a change of tone (Edward R. Murrow). Don't be a sap.

Preparing to alight at Sacramento, adjusting his coat, checking—final private gestures before the public moment

—Mr. Nixon said, "Well, here we go again." This crisp, businesslike exhalation was his only confession of the repetition of things: every day was not different to him. He would now deliver his third major address of the day, but not his last; he had already labored harder than most men labor in a day, and there were sixty days yet before him. I could admire the effort. Given little moments to remember and admire, given a little historical distance, I could write with the ease of detachment.

For the little group of "Nixon Girls" waiting at the Sacramento airport this moment of late afternoon was the day's beginning. They were as fresh and pink as their counterparts had been at Pomona in the morning, San Diego at noon. They presented Mrs. Nixon with roses which soon would wilt and which I would afterward see piled with her wilted orchid and baskets of warming fruit freshly and enthusiastically presented at every seeming destination, places so real and final to the people who came to greet the Nixons, but so indefinite to the Nixons themselves, for whom each destination could only be an illusion of destination. The end was beyond sight; the weariness was here.

Somehow I had never seen the Governor this way, for the Governor never seemed to labor. "I'm going to have a lot of fun this time," the Governor said, but I could not imagine Mr. Nixon's saying that. Often, I thought, Mr. Nixon needlessly punished himself. He worked hard at details that ought to have been beneath his notice, seeming unwilling to delegate even menial authority. The Governor was forever asking, "Where's my briefcase? . . . Where's my speech?" and slapping his pockets, "I had a

[81]

cigar somewhere," or calling, "Where are we? Who are my appointees down here?" trusting someone to know, unlike Mr. Nixon, who served as his own bearer, his own body servant, his own counsel, perhaps out of a servitude I easily recognized because it was so much my own and may have arisen, in his case as in mine, from a projection of his unwillingness to serve others, his jealousy of self, a misguided individualism. My politics was the Governor's collectivism, but I was my own manservant, my own chief clerk, my own research staff, typing all my own manuscripts, and knowing the price I paid in exhaustion for the luxury of my compulsions. I believe in the shorter workweek—for other people.

And again he said, preparing to alight from the bus at Helvetia Park, near Sacramento, "Well, here we go again," walking with reasonable speed across the picnic grounds, shaking hands as he walked, toward the bandstand. *Grove of skyscraping oaks,* I wrote, *whipping wind from mowed field.* Then I thought I'd better know what kind of field it was, and I asked a man who looked rural, and he said it was wheat.

There was something dismal here. It was a bad set for the playwright's play, outdoors and unenclosed, the unconfined crowd appearing sparser than it was, wide-open spaces not only behind the people but between, children running, and the distraction of the odors of the barbecue nearby. It was badly planned. Late as we were, the local chairman nevertheless insisted upon *his* program: this was, after all, *his* moment. He introduced, one by one, with lingering descriptions of the careers they'd left behind, a series of notable figures from the world of sports—an Olympics shot-putter, all-American football players, and several tons of others of whom I had a dim memory and who themselves must have been slightly pained by the contrast between these thrilling accounts of their youth and their present thickly sedentary appearances.

Mr. Nixon, his speech in his hand, stood slightly sheltered from the wind in a hollow near the stairway to the stage, invisible to the crowd and unobserved even by the people surrounding him, who, after all, had already seen him and were now gazing upward at the other celebrities. My own eyes, however, were fastened upon his discomfort. I knew the misery of being made to wait, of being used as a decoy for other intentions. Chilled, perhaps tired, probably hungry, and certainly embarrassed by this evidence of his own powerlessness, a former Vice-President of the United States had a right to complain, to cry out, "Come on, for Christ's sake, put away your shot-putters; make way for the next governor of California."

But it would have won him no friends except me, would have lost him these sportsmen—for this was a rally of "sportsmen," a word not further specified. I tried to show, by some expression of my face, that I sympathized with him, sharing his sense of neglect, but I must have failed, for, although he looked at me, it was without memory. He wanted none of my sympathy.

Neither of us was a sportsman. I knew the boredom of discovering myself in the presence of persons whose ecstasies extend to hunting guns and fishing poles. Guns and poles have no meaning for me; they are not my labor nor my meditation, and I avoided them, as Mr. Nixon avoided them. We had always sat home on our iron butts, scheming how to get ahead of the people who were out fishing.

At last his turn came. "If I have any greater interest than politics," he said, beginning his speech, "it's sports." But it was unbelievable, lacking in all conviction. Endeavoring to imagine Mr. Nixon astride a horse, I arrived at a memory of Thomas E. Dewey in 1944, pretending to be chewing a blade of grass. By some miscalculation, as if a sportsman were not also a citizen, it had been decided to talk here about hunting, fishing, and conservation. But when Mr. Nixon promised a program to increase "catchable trout" there was no response from his audience, nor was the crowd enlivened when, a moment later, he accused the Governor of "running water into the ground." He then promised, if elected, to discharge from public office a certain presumably villainous individual whose name I forget and whose name the sportsmen at Helvetia Park apparently found meaningless, for they persisted in their essential silence, while Mr. Nixon's solitary resonance now began to resemble that of the political orator in Kafka's *Amerika*, of whom the author said that "it was no longer clear whether he was outlining his programme or shouting for help."

Shifting to more familiar topics, he promised to reduce taxes. But in his reversion his sound track automatically added that tax reduction would promote industry in California, this latter portion of his vow logically canceling whatever benefits to sportsmen the former might have produced. Whether the sportsmen noticed I cannot say. It had all begun on the wrong foot, the waning afternoon was irretrievable, and even the promise of "the best Communist control of any state in the U.S." failed to extricate the occasion from the weight of space.

Yet it would be necessary to speak with conviction again tonight, and tomorrow, and in the weeks ahead, to express commitment to a life and a party no longer vividly seen with young devotion. Like an old poet purged of his revolutionary verse, like an actress dead of the weariness of doing again what she had done too often, Mr. Nixon was the living presence, on that windblown stage, of that withering bloom called Early Success. It was the climate of the limbo of all-American football stars, whose lives have no second acts.

Seen in that light, Mr. Nixon was a victim of society about whom I could write with the freedom of my better sympathies. I'd force my compassion upon him. Now I had arrived where I wanted to be. The moon was rising, and the crowd moved toward the food.

But we did not eat, for we had Oakland yet before us. We climbed back aboard the bus, and back aboard the airplanes, winding what we had unwound, pulling up stakes like a road show, without even the help of elephants, once, twice, three, four, five times a day. Pomona seemed continents and ages behind us.

Oakland was another park, but colder here because later and darker, so that when the order was given to shine the floodlights on the crowd, to cheer us up by showing us how many we were, I wished it were heat, not light. Among the people on the stage was John Busterud, who was running for State Treasurer, and who would lose. He was a San

Francisco neighbor of ours—our sons were schoolmates—and his wife, who sat beside him, was very pretty. Though he was bald he wore no hat. I liked his fortitude, I liked his minimal vanity. I thought I'd vote for him. An addled or idiotic fellow with a Polaroid camera came by, selling photographs of the speakers. "Brand new, two bits," he said, and I bought one.

My hands were cold, and I took no notes. I thought I didn't need any, for by now Mr. Nixon's campaign platform was familiar to me.

But what I *did* need was something strong, something good, not from his platform but from him, himself, personally. I needed good "quotes" to balance the good "quotes" I had received from the Governor's own tongue—"Children should lead decent and interesting lives. . . . Liberal government can be responsible government. . . . We pass this way but once, my friend"—things of that sort coming up out of the man's interior, spontaneous, unpremeditated.

The positive aspects of Mr. Nixon, which I intended to employ to balance against my favorable impression of the Governor, had reached me rather through someone else than through him. I realized that Mr. Nixon was preserving two-party government in California, but that had been articulated by Steve Hess, not by Mr. Nixon. The sincerity of Mrs. Nixon told me much about the purity of his following, but that was *her* and *them*, not *him*. My historical tone would give me distance, and I could admire the courage of his stamina, but that was *me*.

Therefore I decided, as a means of drawing him out, to

[86]

ask him a single question testing his capacity to reconcile seeming contradictions between and among three words he used with frequency. I wrote them on my California Legal:

indoctrination   individualism   indecision

In the language of the classroom I would ask him to comment, compare, and contrast, explain his use of. For example, I might ask, "If you favor *individualism* does this conflict with *indoctrination?*"

Or, "In a free society, is *individualism* more or less better served by our toleration for *indecision?*"

Of course, I wanted to be asking, not telling. I didn't want loaded questions. I studied my three words, phrasing questions around them, leaving the bandstand in the park and returning to the warm bus. I sat in the first seat on the right-hand side, beside the window, beside Mr. Nixon's own favorite seat so that he'd have to sit beside me. He couldn't very well pass me by without offending me, and to while away the time I read my Emerson.

CHAPTER 4 ☞

As it happened, however, he rode back to the Edgewater Inn not on the press bus but in a private vehicle, so that I lost sight of him and feared I might not recover it that night at such a sprawling, rambling place—an Inn which was in fact a motel, and at that not a simple motel where people park their cars and go to bed, but a far-flung exercise in a style apparently determined to impose itself upon the whole countryside, for on the following night, on the other side of the Bay, we slept in another motel absolutely indistinguishable from this, my second bedroom absolutely the colors of my first, furnished with the same objects placed in absolutely the same relative positions. Our motels were consistent with political days whose rituals and speeches were more or less identical in roughly identical settings.

I despaired, at the Edgewater Inn, not only of finding Mr. Nixon but of finding anybody or anything, beginning with my own baggage, which I eventually located and wheeled to my room on a handcart identical to that handcart which had been my companion of the night twenty-two years ago, at Meyers Gloves. My assigned room was located in a wing of the motel so remote from the central area that I feared losing contact with the group at large. Mr. Nixon had promised to join the press at its late supper, and I wanted to be there to ask him my semantic questions.

In my room I took time to write briefly in my Journal (". . . Am I prejudiced? . . . He answers questions forcefully, but perhaps evasively, & after I think over what he's said I know he's wrong."), but not to shave—a decision which was to have, I think, a bearing upon events which followed.

Then I set out, losing my way, wandering at last into a linen room where a friendly chambermaid, frowning with uncertainty, guided me down those labyrinths. I walked for a long time behind her. Often she paused at the intersections of corridors, studying the numbers of the doors while thinking backward to occasions when she had been here. She was a traveler to whom the terrain was familiar but not well known, though she had worked here a year. She was a westward migrant to California, from the old country (Arkansas), come in search of bread and butter and her individual identity: when I asked her whom she intended to vote for for governor she offered only a small sigh and said she hadn't began to thank about it, leading me at last to a bright lobby thronging with informed bell-boys who in turn, after several small conferences, directed me to the quarters where my fellow journalists were already eating buffet style, or, frequently, drinking.

The mood was convivial. It might have been a neighbor-hood tavern, except that we were bound not by neighbor-hood but by occupation, and I might have hurled myself into the general laughter except that my day's work was not yet done. For them, each day had its end. There was some satisfaction for me in their growing interest in the nature of my difference from them, stimulated when I mentioned my having once been a newspaperman myself, but escaped. I mentioned having served some months on the ill-fated New York City daily *PM*. Gladwin Hill of the *New York Times* said, "Oh, that Red newspaper," but with a smile, which I returned, to show him I knew he must be joking, for though there had been Reds and Pinks among us we had mostly been, like me, curious and youthful, attracted by a prospectus not less noble than the *Life* prospectus for its California Issue. "We on *PM*," our prospectus roughly read, in part, "are against people who push other people around." I wished that I had shaved, to look less like a Red among these smooth-shaven newspapermen. *They* had shaved, and I felt set apart. It was a scene I knew, a stage-center I did not enjoy but would not relinquish: I was as different now from my fellow workers as I had been different from my fellow workers in the stockroom at Meyers Gloves, doing the same sort of job they were doing, but only for the moment. I was not likely to remain. I was only passing through. It was always understood, in all the shops and factories I had worked, that I should soon depart.

And since I was free in that way, I was also obligated to a task I undertook even in the moment of knowing it would produce pain, chagrin, and embarrassment before resolving itself in the delight of epiphany. Possessing advantages of freedom, I had always been fool enough to stand spokesman for my mates against sergeant or foreman, editor or dean. "Where's the candidate?" I said.

Nobody knew where he was, and since, though he had promised to come, no press release was anticipated, nobody especially cared. Through the smoke they speculated. They speculated that he was resting or that he was conferring with his staff. Nobody speculated that he was drinking, and nobody speculated that he was detained in a linen room with a chambermaid, although of another candidate—a governor, a President, half the Senate, and three-quarters of the United States Congress—they might have indulged all sorts of scandalous speculation. Toward Mr. Nixon their speculations were sober, humorless, restrained, free of cynicism. Even here, in their relaxed hour, off the record, with no responsibility to newsprint, they asserted by their solemnity their conviction of his fundamental detachment from ordinary temptation. They capitulated to that estimate of Mr. Nixon shared even by his most innocent admirers, for whom he was the political equivalent of purity advertised but never achieved—the thornless rose, scuffless shoes, dirtless crops, dustless houses, the Sani-Flush millennium: "Make your toilet bowl the cleanest spot in the house." (At Bethlehem Steel, shaking hands, Mr. Nixon was momentarily entrapped against a background of calendar nudes. With a single helpless glance in the direction of photographers, and with instinctive speed, he escaped. It would have made a memorable photograph, if not for publication for somebody's private collection, but the photographers had been retarded by their own incapacity to believe what their public in turn would have disbelieved: Mr. Nixon against a background of naked flesh would suggest fakery, cropped photographs doctored by enemies who were also the enemies of Easter and Mother's Day.)

Thus I should not have been surprised that they rose when he entered, not out of respect for the office he had held, nor as a courtesy to Mrs. Nixon, who accompanied him, but in deference to a mystery to which they gave the benefit of doubt, their respect for the mystery overwhelming their contempt. They stood with their silverware in hand, their jaws still working.

For myself, however, I could pay no such tribute. Expressed in that moment, I remained seated. I meant no deliberate discourtesy; it was only that my reflex failed to command my rising. The mystery had never gripped me that hard, and by the time I might have risen the moment had passed, though not before he saw me sitting while all were standing, nor betrayed the least surprise that one should sit while others stand: I was a type he knew from campaigns before, one who carried a book and shaved poorly or not at all, who probably wore eyeglasses, perhaps not a Red but anyhow something like a Red, often a Jew, one of those hysterical people who react to public issues as if they were *personal* questions. Of course, what I was, then, was a nut, and you never knew if a nut would sit or stand.

For about a minute he remained near the door, where he had entered. Having promised to appear, he had done so, but the spirit of his promise demanded more. Not until someone asked him if he had eaten did he feel himself welcome. Yes, he had eaten, he said, a hamburger, adding something then about tomatoes, how they were best sliced, how you adroitly worded your request to the waiter to get the best possible slicing; there was a trick to it, a strategy, you had to know how to do it, just right—beginning to move away from the door, having planned his course now, moving with Mrs. Nixon beside him, his arm about her, protecting her, or she him, still speaking of tomatoes as he undertook a route which would carry him around, and out. It was one large room, though a partial wall gave the effect of two, effectively segregating the drinkers from the diners without, by the impediment of doors, discouraging free passage from sector to sector. He disappeared beyond the partial wall, into the other sector, past the bartender, past the drinkers.

He was not long there, and when he reappeared he was not talking about tomatoes but about baseball. Somebody asked him if he preferred the Giants or the Dodgers. He announced no preference, but explored in some detail the relative skills of players of both clubs. It was a subject, like education, I knew enough about to know that he knew nothing more than he read in the newspapers. He had rounded the far end of the dividing wall, talking baseball in the tone reserved for tomatoes or catchable trout.

I rose and went toward him to ask my question. "Don't you think . . ." I began, but that was not a question, and I began again. "Do you think . . ." I began. He had slightly slowed. His objective was motion and departure, but he had granted me the courtesy of slowing, and I began a third time. "Sir," I said. It was by no means a word I had intended to use; it surprised him as much as it surprised me, and he rested upon his heels, halting. "Sir, I want to ask you about three words you've been using."

"Oh, yes," he said, and began to move again, as if I were done, which I was not, but he could not move because I was standing directly in front of him, quite blocking his path. To pass me it would have been necessary for him to turn sideways and proceed crabwise, thus betraying his haste. Again he halted.

I said, "At San Diego this noon you equated education with *indoctrination.* . . ."

"I'm speaking of indoctrination against Communism," he said.

"You also favor *individualism.* But isn't *indoctrination* the antithesis of *individualism?*"

"Read up on the Hiss case," he said, his voice confidently raised. He attempted again to resume his motion, depending upon me to understand that his resumption of motion implied that my question was answered.

"I'm speaking about Communism, too," I said, holding my place. "You say you'll prevent Communists from speaking on college campuses. . . ."

"I didn't say Socialists," he said.

"Aren't you meddling in my classroom now? What about *my* individualism?"

"I said tax-supported colleges only, not Socialists, only Communists. . . ."

"I don't care *who*," I said, "I don't care if it's the Ku Klux Klan."

"You should," he said, pointing his finger at me, and with this I fell back, and he passed. How cleverly, how deftly, how with the wiliest retort he had struck Mark The Glove Boy where Mark The Glove Boy most deeply and anciently lived, carrying me back to that night when my politics had begun, when I had seen, or imagined, hordes of anti-Semites at the Empire Race Track. All that had happened in twenty-two years had sprung from the suspicion of that night. Yet even in the involuntary act of falling back I attempted to preserve what I have forever lost—the precise emphasis of Mr. Nixon's powerful sentence: did he say "You *should*," meaning it was my moral duty, or "*You* should," meaning Mark The Hysterical, Red, Book-Bearing, Bearded, Jewish Glove Boy should? Did he mean to tell me (with which I could agree) that the Ku Klux Klan was as evil as Communism, or did he mean to warn me that every man saves his own skin first? If the latter were the case, it was clear that he was unable to grasp the crucial idea that we achieve freedom only by the perilous course of granting it to our enemies—and if he was unable to grasp *that*, no blacker mark could possibly have been scored against his character.

Or perhaps he meant only, in that midnight necessity, to

pass me by any means, to advance toward the door. As I fell back he hurried by without appearing to hurry at all, and I, recovering, my question unanswered, myself insulted, pursued his left shoulder, which was now beyond me, while between us his wife had inserted herself, who in the moment of my falling-back filled the breach, following, moving after him, protecting him, rear guard, intervening between him and pursuit, so that I could not now overtake him except by shouting at him or by the radical violence of flinging his wife aside, leaping past her, seizing his retreating shoulder, and against his momentum wheeling him about, forcing him to confront me, forcing him to carry our conversation to a natural end, forcing him to stand motionless, like a chastised student, and by an exertion of intellect separate my question from my example, not to obscure my question by fastening upon my impulsive, reflexive metaphor. He reached the door. Turning, and waving his hand to the assembly at large, he smiled, as if he had never had a better time, and was gone.

I do not clearly recall my own actions during the next few minutes. I know I went back to the table for my Emerson, and I think, too, that I ate my unfinished meal, but I may be mistaken in that because I remember being hungry later and accounting for it by recalling that I had eaten only a scattered lunch at San Diego, and an incomplete supper. The newspapermen offered no comment upon my encounter. I thought they were being kind to me, as perhaps they were, though there was also in their attitude the satisfaction of my having learned what they had long ago known—that you couldn't get to him and that there wasn't any point in trying, that his mind was made up. And I could translate into my own experience the Governor's meaning when he said, refusing to debate with Mr. Nixon, "It would go by his rules. It'd be like going out to play baseball and finding out that somone brought a football instead."

I remember thinking, crossing to my room, how refreshing a plunge in the pool would be, though the evening was cool, nobody was swimming, and the signs posted beside the pool probably said, had there been light enough to read by, No Swimming, it was too dark, too late, too cold, or, more likely, simply that the Edgewater Inn took upon itself no extraneous responsibility; it was no such fool as I. I sat in a straight chair beside the pool while my sweat dried. The action would produce a cold which would hamper me in the writing. A week before, I had sat by a pool at a motel in Modesto, telling the Governor (who had asked, "What do *you* think?") that I opposed the tactics of the N.A.A.C.P. in San Francisco in a controversy over *de facto* segregation. The Governor, defending the N.A.A.C.P., neither misunderstood me nor pretended to, well understanding that I might oppose the action while favoring the principle, possessing—in the famous phrases of Scott Fitzgerald—"the ability to hold two opposed ideas in the mind at the same time [while retaining] the ability to function." I had never sweated in the presence of the Governor. He had never told me to *indoctrinate*. His vision of the end was a vision of due process, delegation of responsibility, and the slow formulation of decision and consensus: he had never told me (Mr. Nixon's remark assumed high meaning now) that my college needed a bigger auditorium. Auditorium indeed! Bigger indeed! Indeed!

But let me not dramatize myself by telling of the torment of that night, for there was none, no solitary pacing, no profound insomnia. I remember sitting in that chair but I do not remember rising from it, and I remember shaving, and shaving again in the morning, and extravagantly bathing, and showering in the morning, all in the hope of accomplishing an altered appearance which would preserve both Mr. Nixon and me from the error of believing that my principles were nothing more than the complaint of a hysteric: I would appear as little hysterical as possible, as little bearded. I would pack my Emerson in my suitcase.

As a boy I had always replayed games won or lost— especially lost—until sleep took me off. I must have done so this night. If I dreamed, I must have dreamed representations of Mr. Nixon's shoulder slammed in my face, of his receding, of his finger pointing, of the intercession of his wife. One thing I would do, I thought—or not do—I'd not talk in metaphor, not offer him a target, a Ku Klux Klan, to attack in lieu of my central point.

Because there *would* be another meeting, as there had always been another game after a game lost. It was only fair.

The moment was to arrive sooner than I could have hoped.

In the morning, when he appeared, I was waiting. We were about to speak when he was diverted by a man towing a fiber-glass elephant. (*Life*, for some reason, changed *fiber glass* to *plastic* in a battle yet to come.) Mr. Nixon stood for photographs with the elephant, and my moment, though

I hovered, was lost. On the bus I was unable to seat myself near him, and soon afterward we boarded airplanes at the Oakland airport, our destination Eureka.

I was not in Mr. Nixon's plane but in the following plane, the press plane—we who had lost by lot—aloft only a quarter-hour when our pilot announced that because of motor trouble or some other unspecified mechanical difficulty, Mr. Nixon's plane was returning to Oakland, and we would follow.

Fearful of flying to begin with, I detested turning back. Unable to appreciate the principles by which an airplane flies, I was certainly unable to believe it could continue once disabled: Mr. Nixon's plane would simply stop, like my Japanese car six weeks ago near Yuba City. Mr. Nixon's death a reality now, I made plans accordingly. I would telephone my wife, assure her I was safe, and swear never to fly again. But I regretted not having seen my story through, my not having discovered for myself the truth of him, my not having come to terms with him. An airplane crash, like assassination, settles nothing.*

And so, having killed him once with a revolver and twice by airplane, I saw him next alive as ever on the airfield at Oakland, his plane having been wheeled away for repair and another summoned. I saw Steve Hess hurrying off, and I started after him, hoping he could explain Mr. Nixon's unwillingness to explore my three words with me, hoping he could assure me that Mr. Nixon last night had simply been extremely weary, extremely harried, under dreadful

* Clem Miller, a California congressman, died campaigning by airplane. However, his name remained on the ballot, and he was reelected.

pressures. But Hess disappeared before I could overtake him—into a telephone booth, I later learned, to work in perfect privacy on the day's speeches—and I returned to the landing-strip where Mr. Nixon, with a yellow pencil in his hand (I remember that), was at the center of the cluster of newspapermen, all huddled, shipwrecked, themselves in turn the center of a vast expanse of cement stretching to the wire fences where people had begun to gather in the hope of a glimpse of the former Vice-President of the United States, now candidate for governor of California.

Penetrating the cluster of newspapermen, I worked my way slowly toward Mr. Nixon, who was speaking, and whom I wished to overhear. Soon I caught his tone. It was a neutral topic, like baseball, sliced tomatoes, catchable trout. Specifically, he was dwelling upon the subject of airplane failures, motors gone out, forced landings he had known. He had had four such experiences, and he was telling when and where they occurred, exhausting all detail as a means, I suppose, of controlling the topic. It was the dueler's privilege, choice of weapon, and Mr. Nixon's weapon was trivia. Those newspapermen who had been aboard the Nixon plane offered those of us who had not their notes upon the event, precipitating among us a jovial mockery of the trade: "Was the candidate visibly shaken?" someone asked.

"No," came the reply, "the candidate was not visibly shaken. He was calm and unruffled."

"Was there evidence of panic aboard?" someone asked.

"No," came the reply, "there was no evidence of panic aboard the disabled craft."

"Has the cause of the trouble been determined?" some-one asked.

"Airlines officials have not yet disclosed the cause of the near mishap," came the reply.

"Sir," I said to Mr. Nixon, for I had reached the center now, "last night our conversation was unfortunately inter-rupted just as we were discussing *indoctrination* and *in-dividualism*. . . ."

"Oh, yes," he said.

"And I've been thinking about *indecision*, too, my third word, and banning Communists from campuses . . ."

"From tax-supported college campuses . . ."

"Yes, and to teach my students about Communism my method would be *indecision*, letting my students arrive at good ideas themselves, not through my *indoctrinating* them."

"Remember, I didn't say Socialists," he said. "I said Com-munists."

"I don't care *who*," I said. "The point is that you're telling me how to run my classroom, it's out of your juris-diction, you haven't the facts, it's like your telling me the other night that we need a bigger auditorium. . . ."

"My goodness," said Mr. Nixon, "you're not comparing Communism to auditoriums, are you?" once again seizing my metaphor, though I had vowed to give him none to seize, and spinning upon his heel now, and striding out of the center of the cluster of men through a path opened for him. His shoulder had slammed in my face again. He strode several feet, reaching the outer rim of the cluster. But now he encountered trouble.

The way which lay before him was difficult, impossible, not a door leading into the night, but a vast expanse of flat cement, nothing between him and the fences and the people at the fences, no logical destination in sight: not even the hero of *The Dark Tower* could have walked so long and so purposeless a walk with grace.

Perhaps I began to follow him. I had no sense of his discomfort, only of my own. My confusion had never been greater than now, in these final moments before its everlasting dissolution. *Listen to us, ask us questions*, he had said, and I shouted after him, "See, see, you say you'll answer questions but you walk away; you walked away last night," and he spun again, back to us now, his relief visible, for now, by his turning, it might have appeared to the gathering crowd beyond the fences that Mr. Nixon had detached himself only for the purpose of demonstrating something that only walking could demonstrate, the essential, illustrative detail of some anecdote with which he was entertaining us. Surely it was that—the fences—which stopped him, the scene, the appearance of loss of command, and he shouted at me, pointing at me, "Don't point, don't point, keep your hands down."

I had not known they were up. I had not known that I was pointing. It is a teaching gesture of which I am seldom aware, recognizable to me mainly from candid photographs sometimes snapped by students. Above all, it belongs to me; it was my father's habit before me, and my son's now, so that Mr. Nixon's attack upon my mannerism struck me as a violation of *individualism*, and I became acutely aware of my hands, lowering them as if, in fact, as a former Vice-President of the United States, he possessed some right to order me to do so. Ralph Crane, the *Life* photographer, who supplied the California Issue with a gratifying double-page photograph of the Governor pointing at Mr. Nixon, told me afterward that he had not been conscious of my hands but of the drained whiteness of my face.

Rejoining the group, Mr. Nixon began to speak, but not to me—to Gladwin Hill of the *New York Times*, as if Hill had asked a question—speaking at length, selecting from the sound track a monologue on the Constitutional control of Communism so broad, so bland, and so general that nobody caring for rational economy could have phrased a question to which Mr. Nixon's present unscheduled oration could possibly have been interpreted as response.

No doubt my color returned to my face. As for my hands, I kept them in my pockets. In any case, my fears fled, my anger fled, my confusion fled, my sense of insult dissolved, and all my sense of mystery was dispelled. How could I have feared him or been angered by him or confused or insulted or mystified when there was so little there?

For the truth of Mr. Nixon was really so very simple the student of American civilization should have recognized it sooner: Mr. Nixon was not wicked or evil or malevolent except to the extent that these defects of character arise from low intellect.

Mr. Nixon lacked the self-awareness which intellect produces. He did not know, though he had almost touched upon it at Pomona, that the failure of his language was directly traceable to his lacking a reason to be against those he was against. Empty of response, he walked away, or he told you to put your hands down. His reason for running for governor was the hope of his own success, and he believed success was enough because nobody had ever told him otherwise. He possessed no farther vision of the end. Nobody had ever warned him that the enunciation of a world view toward the end of a private ambition was a torture of credibility which the English language would never contain. Under sufficient, prolonged exposure his reason was bound by stages to fade and vanish.

Had Mr. Nixon been sufficiently self-aware to pursue his inward windings to the discovery of true reasons, he might have forced the Governor to ever-higher purpose by the magical stimulation of critical agreement. He might have been a loyal opposition. There were good reasons for being against those whom Mr. Nixon was against. I knew of several. Steve Hess knew more, and Mr. Nixon could read Hess's reasons in public places when Hess wrote them out. But Mr. Nixon could not feel them, as an actor must *feel* his part, nor utter them unaided, for he lacked the ability to hold two opposed ideas in his mind at the same time.

One idea was the idea of public policy. The other idea was the idea of private success. He could not disentangle one from the other, forbidden by necessity, like the dullest retail merchant, from distinguishing between the object which is of high quality and the object which is merely a popular purchase. Mr. Nixon was unaware that private success might exist side by side with public loss, for he was of the breed of American Success, whose standard was quantification, election, publicity, the certification of numbers, and the adoration of the majority. He knew no other.

CHAPTER 5 ☞

       Thereafter, he smiled quite agree-
ably at me, and I smiled quite agreeably at him in return.
Getting on and off buses and on and off airplanes he was
normally cordial, glad to have me along. He called me by
name. He had taken some further interest in me now, apparently having made inquiries about me, for he told me he
had every intention of reading my books, though I wondered whether, with their oblique style and approach, they
would not be strikingly incongruous among the straightforward, clear, uncomplicated books on Mr. Nixon's
shelves.

  It was pleasant to have a new friend. Nothing can be

sweeter than reconciliation, tranquil peace after discord. For me, the emotion of meeting Mr. Nixon was over, done, this aspect of my job at an end, and I knew what I knew, however uninteresting it may have been, or however little startling it might have been to worldly persons more accustomed than I to the discovery of low intellect in high places.

But I still required, if not for my article at least for my own satisfaction, an event which would correlatively support my discovery, a word, a phrase, an incident, an occurrence, a proof I knew I should discover if I clung long enough and listened hard enough and allowed my mind to wander freely enough among the shower of symbols flying off everything. It would come to me in a moment of repose, no doubt, when I was looking another way and least expecting it. I had hoped to go home to begin writing, but now I planned to remain a while longer, more or less aimlessly tagging along, taking fewer notes in scanter detail, nursing my cold, swallowing Vitamin C. We flew out of Oakland finally, first to Eureka, then to Chico, little cities of northern California.

Arr Eureka 1:05, say my notes, the manly contemplation of the whole (Emerson). Nixon: "Well, hi, are these children yours? Sorry to be late, but the main thing is, we got here." Lumber country, mainly redwood, also fir, bus on the Redwood Highway. White French poodle with Nixon sign. Nixon: "There's a smart dog." Arr 1:30 parking lot 8th and F streets. (Dog was male.) The Flying Supervisor Clausen introduced, flies around everywhere. Clausen: "The State of California is in a financial mess." Nixon: praises the weather, wants to "get on down the road" to Chico (old figure, new vehicle, no roads in the air). Pat N. campaigning this afternoon in Santa Rosa. Nixon: "If you're satisfied with the way things are, then I'm not your man." Individuals, not govt. (good applause). Bystander says: "This man's got so much stature it's pitiful." Bystander voted for JFK but "not so sure" he likes Brown, "too bumbling, doesn't come across to me."

KVIQ-TV in little hotel, sat on bed. Nixon on Birchers: "I have made my position very clear." "In a campaign you've got to expect things from the past to be drug up." Talks to camera, never to man. Asked about "chances." "Very objectively, the race is even now but we're going to pull ahead."

KIEM-TV in big barn studio. Left at 2:50. Shook hands with the help at the airport, found a dollar bill on the ground, went back to the coffee shop. Nixon: "Put it in the tipping money." Nixon to a man: "Tell your mother I'm sorry I didn't recognize her." Signed autographs over the fence. Left Eureka 3:40. The cows don't turn their heads when the plane goes off.

Arr Chico 4:30. Posed with small children. Pat already here from Santa Rosa. Nixon to lady with small children carrying Nixon flags: "You're starting them young." Woman: "They're self-starters." It was a rebuke.

My notes amused me without proving anything. *Arr Elks Club 5:05. Mrs. Nixon wearing blue. Master of ceremonies introducing Nixon: "The bigger the man, the shorter the introduction,"* but even at that it was long enough, and I wandered onto the sidewalk in front of the Elks Club.

[109]

I could hear Mr. Nixon's voice, but I could not hear what he was saying. I wore my WIN WITH NIXON badge, and stood talking with people who, for one reason or another, preferred the outside of the Elks to the inside. I asked why they preferred Mr. Nixon. *Government getting too big,* they said, *taxes too high, too much Welfare, California getting too much like Russia.* I remember best a young woman who told me she favored Mr. Nixon because he would crack down on drug addiction and immorality in the big cities. She was barefoot, wearing shorts so short and a sweater so tight she was scarcely dressed at all, massaging her thighs with the flat of her palms, her costume betraying her inmost soul, all her devils showing, action betraying thought. I went back into the Elks Club. *Receiving line, Mr. and Mrs. Nixon shaking hands, 500 people, pleasantries, "Good to see you again," but not seeing, looking beyond to the end of the line, master of ceremonies herding people through, action betraying thought.*

From the Elks Club I telephoned home to say I was uncertain when I'd return, that I'd discovered something requiring documentation, but that I had no idea when I'd find it since I didn't even know what it was I was looking for.

My aimlessness oppressed me. I detached myself from the Nixon party, bought a large bottle of Vitamin C pills from a druggist who favored capital punishment, and walked several miles at evening up and down residential streets of Chico.

I had never been there. I have not been there since. But I had been in, or worked in, Port Chester and Yonkers and Mount Vernon and Winesburg, small cities resembling

Chico, and I thought I could guess at the life carried on within these houses. Symbols flew off everything—the family car, children's toys abandoned at the supper hour, lawnmowers, the daily newspaper at the door, the evening report on the radio, the mailbox, the milkbox, the doormat, the bell, the knocker, the anachronistic hitching post, the serpentine hose, the rocking chair, garden tools, television antenna, baseball bat, overhead wires carrying the world into the house—all this visible from the sidewalk where I walked and felt, for the first time since accepting this *Life* assignment, a bitterness at the possibility of Mr. Nixon's winning. I did not think he should govern the state where my children were growing, imposing his will upon the people of these houses whose doors without suspicion hung open to the lingering summer, whose own ambitions were so modest they could scarcely have imagined Mr. Nixon's.

Had I described my convictions to Mrs. Queenlee, our housekeeper, she would have said, as she said of all theory, "It's possible." She, too, owned just such a house as these, and having been in hers I seemed to know these.

I did not know how Chico stood politically. I do not know if it gave its majority to Mr. Nixon or to the Governor. On Election Night, when the verdict was certain, I went to bed, caring nothing for the breakdown, then nor ever, satisfied only that something of the feeling I had known on these streets had returned to these houses, gone in through the mailbox, the antenna, come over the wires, because by then I had seen my feeling borrowed by others, my words and phrases borrowed. Under other circumstances I might have resented it.

I could hardly believe, later that evening, in the auditorium at Chico State College, that Mr. Nixon, in a "nonpolitical" speech celebrating Constitution Day, was advocating the suspension of constitutional protection for certain persons who, under certain conditions, refused to answer certain questions. I had expected him, for this night at least, to leave the Constitution alone. The unsteadiness of his position might have been troubling him, for he twice improvised transitions by declaring, "I know that some of you will disagree with me. . . ."

I, for one, disagreed with him, sitting beside Steve Hess in the orchestra pit and muttering my disagreement to him, who told me frankly afterward, on the sidewalk, in the humid night, that my disagreement might not count for much; I was not a significant segment of the population; I was an egghead, and there were only (we guessed, guessing together) a hundred thousand eggheads in California, to which I replied (it was not unclever, I thought) that if it were true, as Mr. Nixon said, that the power of a few thousand Communists was "magnified a thousand fold" it was certainly true that a hundred thousand California eggheads possessed powers of magnification all their own.

It was dangerous, I said, to think of me as an insignificant segment, I was . . . I . . . I think my magnification . . . I think Steve Hess was growing tired of me.

We crossed the street, bought soft drinks from a machine in a gas station, and waited for the campaign bus to load. Hess said I couldn't deny that the meeting had been a great success, a big turnout, much enthusiasm, and I said Yes, I couldn't deny it.

[112]

However, a strange thing was happening. The crowd in the auditorium, instead of bursting into the night with the event upon its lips, was straggling forth in little groups in sodden silence. It was poor management. Mr. Nixon's speech, instead of providing a dramatic conclusion to the evening, proved to be introductory to a tenor who sang a medley of songs describing a musical history of America, from "Yankee Doodle" forward. The crowd, detained by this unexpected pleasure, and finding itself at captive leisure, emerged in a frame of mind more sober than it would have been had the event ended with cheers for Mr. Nixon. He had, in fact, with his final words, made a motion as if to leave the platform. But he had earlier praised the idea of music, and couldn't walk away from it now. He remained upon the stage, taking a seat beside his wife, trapped, I thought, sympathizing with his predicament even as I made my own inconspicuous escape, leaving him to the heat of the auditorium, the late hour, and the prospect of his heavy day tomorrow.

I was waiting in the bus when the newspapermen at last straggled in, some laughing, and some breaking into countersong—Army songs, dirty songs, clean songs with dirty implications—as if to state (for they continued to sing even after Mr. Nixon arrived) that against such purity they would sing their own song, forced into vulgarity by the obscenity of all this patriotic propriety.

They told me that when last seen Mr. Nixon was tapping his foot to the music, and they told me the names of the songs, which I recorded as fast as I could as they shouted them out: *Yankee Doodle, Tenting Tonite, Battle Hymn of*

the R., Dixie, Over There, When J. Comes Marching H.
Again, White Xmas, St. Louis Woman, Anchors Aweigh,
Wild Blue Yonder.

They told me that Mrs. Nixon was tapping her foot, too.
"Tapping both her feet," somebody said.

"Let's be honest," somebody said; "they were both tapping both their feet."

At last the bus began to move, though very slowly
through the crowded streets near the auditorium. Then we
were clear, and the ride to the airport was cool. I put away
my notes. I wanted to relax, uncoil, get a good night's
sleep, and fight my cold.

I sat at the rear of the airplane with Mrs. Nixon and two
women of the Nixon party, one of whom—a tireless sec-
retary—I had read about in *Six Crises*. Her ankle was taped
—she had fallen, I think—and we talked about her ankle
and my cold.

It was the Convair that had broken down that morning.
The Flight Engineer who had repaired it brought us coffee
now, and I asked him if he could tell me exactly what had
gone wrong. He told me, but in a way too complicated for
me to understand, and I asked him if he couldn't reduce it
to a phrase—all I had, I said, was ten pages in space, and I
couldn't go into a whole hell of a lot of areonautical detail.
Sympathetically he crouched beside me, giving the matter
hard thought, and formulating at last a tight, neat phrase—
"malfunction of a prop-control switch"—which I wrote
on the side of the paper coffee cup, thanking him, admiring
him for so succinct an analysis; and Mrs. Nixon said, re-

ferring to the meeting at Chico, "Wasn't that exciting! It was just like a revival meeting."

People have asked me since, Did she really say it or did you make it up? The question angers me. I go by the old rules. But even for me, in this moment of hearing what I expected soon or late to hear, belief was difficult. It was too perfect a proof of intellect, almost too conclusive, supremely expressive of the evangelical faith serving as a substitute for reason when one has no reasons to be against those he is against. Mr. Nixon's wife and principal admirer required neither fact nor logic. If our own age, knowing so much, demands more than simple faith, she at least gave me faith of another kind—a faith in my own theory, my own suspicion of the meagerness of intellect among Mr. Nixon's equipment.

And yet perhaps against the pounding of the airplane, or because of the congestion caused by my cold, I had heard her wrong, and so I asked her, leaning forward, putting my ear close to her, "Like a what?" and she said again, "Like a revival meeting," and I wrote it on my coffee cup below the phrase supplied by the Flight Engineer.

On the following day, somewhat to the surprise of my family, I returned home.

So I sat to write with sixty-two pages of California Legal before me, and the Turner thesis, and one paper coffee cup. As a writer I was not without experience. Yet it is always impossible to begin.

In the present case I was burdened additionally by the

feeling that I was doing two things at once—that I was writing, but that I was also participating in a political campaign. It was a wrong mixture: writing ought to have no objective outside itself, no public purpose. I hoped that as I became immersed in the writing the other consciousness would pass, along with my cold, which was now in its third day, had three days yet to run (based on past performance), and would then settle into a three-week cough.

Past performance ran true. At the end of three days my cold had gone, my cough had come, and I had covered forty pages, opening with the Turner thesis and moving as fast as I could along the general lines of my outline, trusting my momentum to discover what was there, depending upon the prose to shape and select its tone and images, I to follow along with the deepest interest. After a while I would call a halt, end this free play, back up and organize things. I had no choice but to depend upon chance and accident, push nothing, force nothing, abandon any cherished notion at any moment in favor of a lucky jump, and to know by my tension and posture in my chair, or by the beat and pump of my blood, when things were going right or wrong.

It was a process of discovery which produced a splendid collection of matching images like those which had risen from the Frost-Sandburg materials (the Governor as Californian, Mr. Nixon as national; the Governor as incumbent, Mr. Nixon as seeker; the Governor's spending, Mr. Nixon's frugality; the Governor's record, Mr. Nixon's critique), all enwrapped in the voice of the historian trying as hard as he could to be neutral in the future indefinite tense.

After I had forty pages, I set aside my California Legal—

on a high shelf, hard to get at—and consulted only what I had written. My forty pages had replaced my notes, as the notes had earlier replaced the event, reality receded. I hoped within a week to extract from my forty pages ten lucid, coherent sheets of clean prose to send to my editor at *Life.*

At the same time I was aware of no desire so strong as the desire to abandon the whole thing, wanting to quit, wanting to lie in the sun, read a slow book, play with my children, wanting to take up again with my wife where we had left off on the day of our marriage, having become embroiled in the seventeen years since in an ambition not less fierce nor single-minded than the ambition of Mr. Nixon, to rise, to succeed in the public way. I wanted to write with no end in view but inner satisfaction, but I wanted also to please my editor, by way of appearing in the California Issue, by way, in turn, of informing the voters in 1962, and reaching into history besides.

School had opened. I was teaching Emerson, whom I had carried with me to Beverly Hills and back, *via* the fairgrounds at Pomona, the Palm Room of the U. S. Grant Hotel, the Edgewater Inn, and points north; Benjamin Franklin; Mark Twain's *Life on the Mississippi,* Henry Adams, Scott Fitzgerald—a book of each, each an American success story—and *No Further West,* by a South African named Dan Jacobson, a book about the freeways of California, about that abundance over which we had flown, and the institutions we had encountered. No wonder the course was called American Values, by whose end I should also introduce to my students an article from *Life* on Mr. Nixon and the Governor, which the teacher himself had written and could therefore discuss from a point of peculiar vantage.

My writing day was foreshortened, but that was well. It was an old story with me. Prevented from going too far upon any one night, I was coerced rather into thought than verbiage, each session at the writing followed by a period of enforced cooling off. It was well to retard things, avoid quick decisions, prevent decisiveness.

I reduced my forty pages to fifteen, submitting these to my wife, who, according to my Journal, pronounced them "more than adequate but less than brilliant," whereupon I rewrote them, hoping to maintain the adequacy while climbing to brilliance, though when it was done my wife said she couldn't see how it was any different from before. I assured her it was, and mailed it away.

That was a Wednesday, and I thought I was done. I was satisfied to settle for mere adequacy in view of my having carried out the intention I had begun with—to be fair, to remain neutral, to restrain my prejudices, to be just. It was a journalistic ideal, a historical requirement, and probably a psychological impossibility, and I had evidence that I had come close to it: on Friday night Herbert Gold, the novelist, came to the house, bringing with him a former book reviewer named Mike Grieg, who, in the process of writing a novel, was discovering how much more difficult writing was than reviewing; and a fellow whose name I never caught who kept referring to President Kennedy as "Jack" so we'd all know—well, you know what. We were joined by a neighbor and by my wife, though at the height of the evening my wife left to console a lady crosstown whose lover had died that morning in Salt Lake City in the arms of a wife we had never known he had. We talked about that, and about Cuba, and about the Giants and Dodgers who were still deadlocked, and about Mr. Nixon and the Governor. Gold had taken the carbon copy of my manuscript into a corner with him, and returned to say it was "too fair."

How could anything be "too fair"? It was like being "too healthy." It reminded me of a college president for whom I once worked who sneered at students who were "over-intellectual."

Gold cited in particular a passage he objected to on the grounds it made Mr. Nixon "a real hero." I had written:

> In law school Mr. Nixon once heard advice he never forgot: the secret of success is "an iron butt." Mr. Nixon had it. On his airplane flights, though his only privacy was a swivel-seat, he contrived to disappear utterly into his own work. To the cabin behind him only the top of his head was visible. His lap was his desk. . . .

"I identify with him," I said to Gold somewhat defensively. But possibly I had overcorrected. Fearing my prejudices, perhaps I had gone too far the other way.

Had I been too fair? I fretted away the weekend, fearing I had so far balanced my emotions that I had scored too heavy a triumph over the scandalous prejudices inherited from Mark The Glove Boy. I read my article half-a-dozen times at least. True, it was adequate but not brilliant, and perhaps too little weighted: as reader, as voter, I was uncertain what values the writer awarded the images he had selected. Half-a-dozen readings did not help, nor would half-a-dozen more.

On Monday morning David Maness telephoned from *Life*. He was not an editor I had yet worked with, but he had a high title—Articles Editor—and therefore appealed to my vanity. His New England accent was extremely pleasant. I coughed for a while, and apologized. "There are a lot of them going around here, too," he said. As for the article—there's something wrong with it, he said.

"That's what my wife says," I said. "It's two to one against me now."

"Either way you'll have a World Series out there," he said.

"I hope you don't have a lot of work in mind," I said. "What do you think's wrong with it exactly?"

Maybe talking about it we'd find out what, he said. The opening was fine, he said, "the long view very important." I wrote it on my California Legal. It opened fine and ended fine and the historical perspective was quite O.K., but what was needed was—landmarks.

"Landmarks," I said, coughing, and writing it down. Somewhere in my own vocabulary I had a word meaning the same thing, and we talked in the hope of finding it, without doing so, though it didn't matter, for in the course of talking we discovered the trouble: it needed work, one more going-through and one more coming-out, one more stage of evolution, one more hard look at every connection, one more thorough writing and retyping and wringing and drying; time and work.

I took down from the shelf my sixty-two pages, and my forty pages, and my fifteen pages, cutting my fifteen pages into strips and ribbons, tenatively hanging them together with Scotch tape, and finally more permanently bridging them with borrowings from the earlier materials. In the main, I built up the middle, though at the end I now permitted the historian two departures from his earlier objectivity: he rather scoffed at Mr. Nixon's notions of individualism, and he summarized the intellectual spirit of the Nixon camp by recording Mrs. Nixon's allusion to the revival meeting. This done, her allusion struck me as too sudden, lacking in dramatic preparation, so I bolstered the moment by providing her with her earlier exclamation, "Hasn't it been exciting!"

It was a lot of work. I copied it over once more—once extra—tampering beyond reason, and mailed it back. On the following Monday—October 8th—Maness called again, saying, "You're fine," meaning, I thought, it was done, we were in, though there would undoubtedly be, he warned me, some last-minute cutting for space. "The cutting going on around here is brutal," he said.

"I'll sit by the phone," I said.

My article was to "close," as they say, two days later.

A few hours after my happy conversation with Maness I received airmail special delivery from *Life* a Working Draft of my article—simply a duplication of my manuscript for distribution to many points of the *Life* office, where many minds (I don't know how many; say ten) test it from many viewpoints, where a wise elder would shrewdly question whether Mr. Nixon's audiences "could not" or

"did not" cheer the gas chamber, where another would react to my punctuation, where someone else would cross-
check my arithmetic, somebody here or there polish a passage (I'd pretend the change was a typist's error and restore
my own), and somebody else introduce an expository phrase
for the benefit of millions of readers less close than I to the
California situation. Someone would telephone me to debate
the use of "each" as opposed to "both," while somewhere
in some hidden recess of the *Life* office somebody without
notification to anybody else was transforming my *fiber-
glass* elephant to *plastic*.

My manuscript had spawned ten of itself—my magnification was tenfold and just beginning—each Working Draft
identical to my manuscript, but with altered pagination.
Therefore it was visually different, no longer quite my own,
and as I read it I had the feeling that terrible, brutal cuts
had been made. Yet when I compared it to my manuscript
I saw that nothing was missing; it was as I had sent it.

But something *was* wrong that worried me now. It was
the whole damn look of the thing that worried me now.
Somehow it had moved beyond me in a strange way more
than visual. We had done well to impose upon it one more
evolution; it was more adequate, it was still fair—I could
see where it *had* improved—but the new strength had introduced new problems. The beginning and the end, which
against the weak middle had looked so fine a week ago, now
looked absurdly underdeveloped. What now? Development
would increase length at the moment everybody at *Life*
was crying about space. I didn't care.

Therefore I decided to change the viewpoint from that

[122]

of "the historian" to "I . . . me," as the only possible means of achieving conformity of tone and viewpoint, much to the surprise of David Maness, to whom I spoke Tuesday after working far into the night Monday.

"I shudder at the prospect of having it retyped and submitted to all hands again," he said.

"It's only pencil work actually," I said.

"It dawns on me now," said Maness, "that—as we insert these personal pronouns . . ."

"I'm saving you terrific space," I said. "But if we're going to save space we better make it look like we did it purposely, not just for *space*."

"Isn't it becoming a very personal sort of thing?" asked Maness.

"But it looked worse with that historian suddenly coming back from the future for coffee with Mrs. Nixon," I argued.

"You might be right," he said.

"And we'll be changing the tense, too," I said, "from the future indefinite . . ."

"The what?" he said.

"To the present past," I said.

Soon we had won space without losing stylistic consistency. We reached good agreement. I thought it was less than my best writing—that it never *would* be brilliant in the literary way of my wife's desire—but I thought, too, that in a big, colorful, splashy California Issue it might pass unnoticed. Maness would submit it elsewhere in the *Life* office and call me back if there was any "balking."

"I'll sit by the phone," I said.

[123]

That was Tuesday, and he did not call. I heard only from a Miss Silva, who asked me whether I had actually *heard* all the utterances I had quoted. Perhaps she was referring to my little scene with Mrs. Nixon. I never knew. I replied in a superior tone, "Well, I would never put a quote in unless I had heard it." Our conversation was very brief.

On Wednesday morning, arising at seven, I telephoned Maness, for whom it was midmorning and who, since this was closing day, would be under some pressure. I hoped the pressure would work to my benefit, but I couldn't know—the styles of editors vary. Our conversation, which cost us —cost him, cost *Life*—$45.45 plus tax, was almost entirely congenial. We talked tenses, pronouns, fiber-glass elephants, punctuation, quotation marks, and capital letters. I objected to several non-words *Life* hoped to insert, granted the non-word "just-built," and reduced by $25,000,000 (it was nothing) my estimate of the cost of the Governor's Water Plan.

Then we arrived at trouble. Maness objected to my first reference to Mrs. Nixon—"Hasn't it been exciting!"—and I fought for it upon the grounds that it established the necessary dramatic precedent for the second reference, my most telling line of all, the summation of the spirit of Mr. Nixon's campaign, my scoop, my discovery, my proof.

"No, that's all right," Maness said, "because we're taking the second one out, too."

Sic semper tyrannis! David. So they didn't believe it, either, as I hadn't believed it, and had had to ask again! But wasn't that all the more reason to retain it? Now I knew its absolute importance. "Well, I'll tell you, David," I said

—though I'd been calling him "Mr. Maness"—"that's the one thing I'll absolutely have to insist on. If we kill that, we might as well kill the whole article."

There was a protracted silence. Perhaps it was a five-dollar silence.

Eighteen years before, at Port Chester, for the *Daily Item*, I had covered a luncheon speech by a certain citizen of the Village, who expressed, in the course of things, his son's gratitude for the gift of tobacco sent to him by the Port Chester Service Man's Cigarette Fund, the country then being at war, and the son serving. With all good will I wrote the statement into my story.

But the man complained to my editor, Ed Hughes, that he had said no such thing, that his son could not possibly have received the gift of tobacco since he was a resident elsewhere than Port Chester, nor could the son's name, by any ingenuity, have worked its way onto the lists of the Fund, although it was undeniably true that the father, in addition to other civic duties, served also as a functionary of the Fund.

The father demanded a retraction, and when I refused to retract he threatened me with legal action, hinting also at bodily harm. I wished no part of either, and I walked in caution for several weeks, locking my rooming-house door, fearful enough, but insufficiently fearful to write a craven retraction of words I knew I had heard and knew I had not written in malice (for I had not had the least idea where his son resided).

The father's threats increased in anguish until my editor, weighing the simple annoyance of the situation against the fragility of my boyhood pride, urged me for his sake, if not for God's truth, to write out a brief retraction. With much mumbling, I did so, the father's ringing of our telephone came to an end, but my remorse only to its beginning, as of a wrong committed, as of something stolen and never returned, a small crime whose memory curls my lip in the act of my writing, making me still wish to undo something which, in the scope of things, so little matters. But having done it I was never, in my own mind, completely or scrupulously successful, as I should now certainly fail of success and fall beyond redemption forever if I agreed to the proposed deletion.

"You feel *that* strongly," Maness said.

"Stronger," I said.

"We'll see if there's any balking," Maness said.

"I'm really sorry," I said, and I really was. He had his job, and I had mine. I should have hated not to appear in the California Issue, having told all my friends to look for me, and having written, I thought, the fairest, best journalistic account of the race for governor of California in 1962.

"Sit by the phone," said David Maness.

There was no call. I assumed my article closed. There was a telegram Thursday saying we had closed. I assumed Mrs. Nixon had closed with it.

I found storage space on my shelves for my California Legal, my forty pages, the strips and ribbons of my second draft, my third draft, the Working Draft, notes covering the telephone conversations. I might never need these pages again, but I could not part with them. The sight of them, from time to time, would instantaneously re-create the ex-

pulence of these two months, be my pay long after my pay was spent. They were the experience I had bargained for on the telephone from Nevada City.

Heavy rains began in San Francisco. During the weekend the roof of my study sprang leaks, and I covered things with the newspapers I had bought in quantity during the weeks I had been working on the article. The World Series— Giants and Yankees—returned from New York but couldn't play. Saturday was our third day of rain. Sunday the sun was bright, but Candlestick Park was wet.

On Monday they played. It was the sixth game, and I went, carrying *Life on the Mississippi* and arriving early, and reading for two hours while helicopters fanned the field, drying it. There was a left-field helicopter, a center-field helicopter, and a right-field helicopter. Today or tomorrow the Series would end, and the campaigns would receive a greater share of public attention. Tomorrow the California Issue of *Life* would appear on the newsstands, and I could not prevent myself from thinking about Mr. Nixon as, beneath the drone of the helicopters, and amidst the color and flutter of the arriving crowd, I came upon a passage in *Life on the Mississippi* which, for exactitude, surpassed the sum of what I had done or what anybody else had done, or what anybody was likely to do. "The Model Boy of my time . . . was perfect," wrote Mark Twain, "perfect in manners, perfect in dress, perfect in conduct, perfect in filial piety, perfect in exterior godliness; but at bottom he was a prig; and as for the contents of his skull, they could have changed place with the contents of a pie, and nobody would have been the worse off for it but the

[127]

pie. This fellow's reproachlessness was a standing reproach to every lad in the village. He was the admiration of all the mothers, and the detestation of all their sons. I was told what became of him, but as it was a disappointment to me, I will not enter into details. He succeeded in life."

It was the first World Series I had attended in twenty-six years. It had been my fourteenth year; I had arisen at three o'clock of a Saturday morning, walked through Mount Vernon to the Bronx line, and traveled by subway to Yankee Stadium. My companion was a boy named Norman Apell, who, within a decade, would die in Normandy. We stood in line for hours. I carried my lunch in a shoebox, and a book to read. It was Joe DiMaggio's freshman year, and Bill Terry's last; others who played in that game that day— Ott, Lazzeri, Gehrig—are dead.

The Giants lost the game after two Yankees were out in the eighth inning, in a moment painful to recall. With the score tied, and Yankees on first base and third, Crosetti hit a ball which the Giants pitcher, Fitzsimmons, could neither field nor avoid, with the effect of simply slowing it, while Burgess Whitehead, the Giants second baseman (a special hero of mine, for he was said to be learned), in a heroic contortion, flung himself at the slow-rolling ball, and in a desperate motion doomed to fail threw it to first base weakly and too late. From third base the winning run ran home.

I had been sitting in the bleachers that day in 1936. Now, in San Francisco, Mark The Glove Boy had advanced to the grandstand. The Giants scored early and commanded throughout. Thus the game lacked excitement, although, as always, there was a moment worth the price—Willie Mays racing from first base to third after a bad throw by Whitey Ford, dashing out from under his hat, his face set, my heart leaping. I was in a perfect position to see his face as he came, this moment of pure effort, like the heroic contortion of Burgess Whitehead, this absolute allegiance to a present purpose, to a decision carried through without the contemplation of ulterior possibilities, without equivocation or doubt or question, with a clear mind knowing all its own motives, knowing what must be done, and doing it with all haste. As Emerson's style was my consolation, so was the style of Willie Mays after two months among the evasions of political language.

Once, for *Life*, I had written an article about Mays, but it had gone poorly, and my editor and I agreed to abandon it. Between Mays and me there had been mistrust. Though he gained confidence in me as we proceeded, we never recovered from the disbelief with which he had first greeted me. He had said: "Go ahead and write it, just go ahead and write what you want. That's what you guys do anyhow."

Had I, in the present case, in tomorrow's article, done more than that? Had I written only what I had wanted to write, or had I really discovered what the candidates were like? Had I objectified them, or had I simply written down my prejudices? It was beyond me now to know. Now it would be public, and in an odd way public judgment would itself form mine.

As a literary standard such a judgment violated my senses. But, then, my article had failed of literature, as my wife had told me from the start. Or even if, by some standard more lenient than hers, it *were*, it was still something else as well: with Election Day only three weeks away, and the distractions of baseball at an end, it was inevitably a campaign document bearing upon events with a force even greater than numbers suggest, though the numbers themselves were, impressive: *Life*, according to a trustworthy estimate, sold 1,400,000 copies of its California Issue in California.

I always buy an excessive number of copies of any magazine containing samples of my writing. I usually buy them, as I bought the California Issue, at Edna's and Jerry's Toys, a neighborhood establishment where my children and I have spent many happy hours, they at the toys, I at the reading (at the "books," as they are called, though in fact they are magazines), where one may also purchase from a selection of religious trinkets and reproductions and crucifixes with realistic blood. The outstanding paradox of America is nowhere more vividly underscored than here, in our Catholic neighborhood, where the tokens of religious devotion are displayed without conscious tension among hundreds of magazines eclectically ranging from those which will interest an immigrant Italian lady dressed in mourning for her husband twenty years dead (a laborer he was, no doubt, who had paved the streets outside) to her son, who has become physician, physicist, priest, or even intellectual, such is the rate and the variety of our neighborhood.

My memory of my first reading of my article is accompanied by pains in my thighs, for I read crouching, not intending to read it through, only to check upon the two sequences with Mrs. Nixon, which were in place, but subtly altered. I had written, "Hasn't it been exciting!" *Life* printed, "Hasn't it been exciting?" I had written, "Wasn't that exciting!" *Life* printed, "Wasn't that exciting?" My whole point was that she had exclaimed, not asked. I was dismayed, yet also too fascinated to rise from the rack, too impatient, after all, even after twenty years of writing, and so I remained crouched, absorbed. This is the article I read:

Where is California going? What is the animating impulse beneath the inert statistics? How is the human heart of California shaped? What are its desires, its fears, its values? Two California men have been laboring harder than all others to find the answers: Edmund G. Brown, a Democrat, governor of California for four years, and Richard M. Nixon, a Republican, who was Vice President of the United States for eight. On Nov. 6 the people of the state are to elect one man governor and return the other to private life.

They bear certain resemblances. Both are self-made men, lawyers, husbands, fathers, natives of California born in this century. Both now seek an office paying $40,000 a year, though each could command much more money with less labor and much less abuse in private practice. In their public lives, however, history has led them separate ways. And it occurred to me that in its weighting of this difference between the two men California's story might tell itself.

Governor Brown for 12 years has served Californians as an officer of the state. Mr. Nixon has never held state office. Presumably the governor's knowledge of state affairs runs deep. Presumably Mr. Nixon would infuse state affairs with the broad outlook of his 14 years in Washington.

Broadly speaking, the governor is a "bread and butter" man who favors the extension of government service as the most stable guarantee of individual comfort. Mr. Nixon holds that the best government is one which governs as little as possible.

Governor Brown is California's heir to the New Deal, the Fair Deal and the New Frontier, hailed by a partisan orator as a man who embodies "the political sagacity of Franklin Roosevelt, the fighting heart of Harry Truman, and the forward look of John F. Kennedy." Dwight Eisenhower, in a telegram to Mr. Nixon, expressed "my full confidence in you as a person, as a candidate, and as admirably equipped to be the next governor of California."

I had heard the candidates call one another "great" and "distinguished," and I hoped to find greatness and distinction in them. I could forgive them their rhetoric when it was merely conventional and seek behind it the language of wisdom. I would forgive Governor Brown and Mr. Nixon the pure whites and the pure blacks of political persuasion. (Spurning a black Stetson offered to him at a rally in the Mother Lode country, the governor objected, "The bad guys wear this. I'm the good guys." Replying to implications in a newsman's question about his brother Donald, Mr. Nixon, at one stroke dissolving all the labyrinths of motivation, asserted, "I am an honest man.")

At the outset the lines of battle were drawn in patterns

prescribed by the logic of politics. This much could have been guessed. Governor Brown would defend his record of office: "California was never more prosperous, and her future never brighter. We have had no new taxes in three years, we have had four consecutive balanced budgets, and we have done all this by playing fair with the taxpayer's dollar." Mr. Nixon attacked: "I see the billboards of my opponent, 'Keep California first.' Yes, California is first in taxes, first in spending, and first in crime." The principal task of the candidates was to locate the winning issues, find their themes. Whether these were the issues and themes mankind would ultimately perceive as most fateful, I could not know. What mattered to the candidates now was the volume of the crowds' cheers, the energy of the crowds' applause, the captivating simplifications which could rouse campaign workers and send them forth radiating enthusiasm and ringing doorbells.

Each candidate got his campaign under way from a familiar site—Governor Brown on a raw, cold evening at Union Square in San Francisco; Mr. Nixon on a damp, foggy morning at the fairgrounds of Pomona, in the southern portion of the state.

True to all the success books from Benjamin Franklin to Horatio Alger, each candidate was a man of humble origin. Nor did he conceal it. Here on the streets of San Francisco, Governor Brown had peddled newspapers. Here he had studied law and been elected to his first public office. Successively district attorney for San Francisco County, then attorney general for California, he had been elected governor in 1958 by a margin of more than a million votes.

Mr. Nixon had delivered groceries from his father's store in Whittier, 20 miles from Pomona. From this district he had gone to Congress. From here he had begun his campaign for Senator in 1950, and for Vice President in 1952. Once in the nation's No. 2 office, he had become an international figure, moved to the head of his party's ticket in 1960, come within just 119,000 votes of the presidency.

"Tonight," Governor Brown said at Union Square, "we step into the ring for the main event." He announced that he had lost 18 pounds, wishfully adding that a man so well disciplined "ought to be elected by acclamation." He alternately likened himself to a salesman ("I'm selling my record. It's a good product and the people are going to buy it. We have made good on our promises") and to a lawyer ("When I was lawyer, I went into court knowing if I had a good case, a fair case, or a poor case. In this campaign I've got a good case").

At Pomona, where cheerleaders led a waiting crowd with the chant, "Nixon is blue hot" (to avoid the word "red"), Mr. Nixon, arriving by helicopter, said, "We're going to travel more miles and make more speeches and shake more hands than any candidate in the history of California." He promised that, if elected, he would serve a full term: ". . . I make that pledge, here in this district, today." (Governor Brown, who disbelieved him, parodied a primer for children: "Dick sees the big house. 'Oh, what a pretty house,' said Dick. 'It is big and pretty and white. It is called the White House.' Dick said, 'How I would love to live in the big White House.' But Jack lives in the White House.")

Mr. Nixon complimented the cheerleaders, the brass

band, local Republicans, the mayor of Pomona, and "the best fair in the United States." Quoting a Democrat who had predicted "the dirtiest campaign" in California history, Mr. Nixon said, "Well, if this is a dirty campaign it will be because they make it so." He would fight clean, he said. There were things he would not mention. For example, he would not mention (mentioning it) four relatives of Governor Brown in state employ. Mrs. Nixon was introduced as "the woman who's going to remodel the governor's mansion." ("What does [Mr. Nixon] want with the governor's mansion," the governor countered, his opponent's just-built home in mind, "with his seven bathrooms and his six crises down there?")

At Salinas an undergraduate asked Governor Brown, "Why are you here?" The Governor's reply was straightforward enough. "I'm here to get the people to re-elect me governor," the governor said.

The student persisted: "What are the issues?"

"My record is the issue," the governor replied. "First come the bread-and-butter issues—profits for business and jobs for workers. Then education, water, fair employment, social welfare and the fight against crime."

Later his "points for progress" would find that order slightly revised but the emphasis the same. "Listen," said Governor Brown, "here's the problem of the average fellow making his living in California: he's growing lettuce in his backyard, and he's asking himself a question—'How am I going to water it, and will a freeway run through it?'"

Water, obviously, was to be a basic issue even in an ultramodern California whose apparent life was freeways, missiles, oil and wine. The California Water Plan, a $1.75 billion irrigation, conservation and recreation project ("the largest water project in the history of man," said Governor Brown), was the achievement the governor was proudest of. Without a proper distribution of water, he maintained, it was absurd even to speak of a future for California. "We've got 1,700 people a day coming to California, and none of them bringing their own water."

But his Water Plan was attended by the threat of political consequences in the northern counties, where it was feared that diversion to the south endangered sources of supply. Thus, one of the governor's principal tasks was to persuade his constituency that his plan served the whole state.

In Modesto the governor toured a cannery, shook hands with ladies on the assembly line, ate a peach and returned to his motel to rest before his evening speech.

To what end all this shaking of hands and slapping of shoulders, this standing for photographs and signing autographs and touring canneries, this flying-in and flying-out of Fresno and Salinas and Modesto, and announcing his weight in every town? Rudely the question was addressed to the candidate: "Governor, what is your vision of the better life?"

It was a question infrequently asked, if at all, during the practical frenzy of this political campaign and the governor lived with it for several moments. Earlier in life the governor might have asked the question of himself; before he became governor he, too, had been introspective—kept a daily diary of his life and from time to time escaped to the solitude of religious retreats.

"My friend," he said, "it's not enough just to be governor, if that's what you mean. If I had to do something that wouldn't let me live with myself afterward, I'd have to say to myself, 'No, Mr. Brown, it's back to private practice for you.' We pass this way but once, my friend.

"I'd say this. I'd say after the bread and butter comes play—more time for play and recreation in God's fresh air, and enough fish in the rivers."

Signing his autograph for a little girl, he compacted his conviction in six words: "Study hard, but play hard, too." And in another moment, still molding his answer to the visitor's question, he said, "Children should lead decent and interesting lives."

At Los Banos the governor ate barbecued steak. As he began his speech, he said: "I am an epicurean, and this is the best dinner I have ever had anywhere, any time, any place in the state of California." His manner was confident. In his buoyant mood he discarded his prepared text and spoke intimately, off the cuff. Departing he observed that the loss of person-to-person contact was a state problem too. "Sometimes," said the governor of California, "I wish I lived in one of those small states you can walk around."

At the fairgrounds at Pomona, after the cheerleaders stepped aside, Mr. Nixon said, "We have got to have a reason to be against those we are against." Facing the realities of bread, butter, water and lettuce, Mr. Nixon's work lay before him. Forswearing pork-barrel promises and compelled by conviction and political circumstance to avoid a "me too" program of expanded welfare, he said, "I am not taking the easy road to win. It's much easier to promise everything to everybody."

Large matters were at stake. If Governor Brown conceived of his own role as the task of "protecting the general populace from people who might overreach themselves," Mr. Nixon's was the historic task of preserving two-party government in California; unchallenged, unrestrained by strong opposition leadership, the Democratic party could overreach itself.

Mr. Nixon's job in 1960 had been to defend an Administration of which he was a part and whose work he viewed as positive. But now, like President Kennedy before him, he was committed to bad news—the unhappy position that affairs had been mismanaged. It was his task to strike the negative note with the positive chord.

At the San Diego airport Mr. Nixon stood for photographs with local candidates. "How's it going?" he asked. Someone replied, "We're running scared and hard."

At lunch Mr. Nixon was introduced by his Republican opponent of the June primaries. Mr. Nixon applauded this evidence of the restoration of party unity and called for a viewpoint which would "look beneath the label and vote the man." In his prepared text he cited rising unemployment in the San Diego area and went on to score "the present state administration" for having "swept the problem under the rug."

In Sacramento he traveled to a sportsmen's rally within a grove of skyscraping oaks. A whipping wind from a mowed wheat field lashed an adherent's sign, "God Save Our State. Down With Brown." Mr. Nixon stood a bit forlorn and perhaps a little neglected, while a gathering of notable sports figures was introduced. Then he praised sports, praised the fighting spirit of the Los Angeles Angels and outlined a recreation program which would, among other things, extend the availability of hunting grounds and "expand the catchable trout program."

"Hasn't it been exciting?" Mrs. Nixon said. I politely said it had. But the day had echoed with negative sounds —the rise in unemployment, the advance of crime, "chiselers" on the welfare rolls and wasted water. Mr. Nixon favored not only the retention of capital punishment but its extension. Perhaps the negative tone was true and right, but the candidate's audience did not cheer the gas chamber, and catchable trout is a secondary crisis.

In this moment Mr. Nixon was revealed less as the hero of a drama than as the author of a play still trying out, still out of town. He was listening from every platform not only for the applause and adoration reserved for heroes and celebrities, but for the cheers he could safely translate into the enthusiasm that heralds the ringing of doorbells and votes.

At Oakland Mr. Nixon stood for his photograph with a 10-foot plastic elephant. It brought him little luck: after a quarter hour in the air, his plane developed mechanical difficulty and he turned back. Someone analyzed the trouble as "a faulty left-wing governor," a quip the candidate offered from the rostrum in Eureka later that afternoon. ("Malfunction of a prop-control switch," said a non-political flight engineer.)

"Sorry to be late," he told his welcoming committee, "but the main thing is, we got here." A lady's white French poodle wore a Nixon jacket. "There's a smart dog," said Mr. Nixon. He spoke to a crowd at a parking lot, whirled through two television interviews and flew out of Eureka 30 minutes behind schedule.

At the Elks Club in Chico he and Mrs. Nixon shook hands with some 500 campaign workers and received a basket of "Paradise apples from Paradise people." A schoolboy in the receiving line, confessing that he was too young to vote, promised to vote for Mr. Nixon for President in 1968. "Attaboy," said Mr. Nixon. "Talk it up."

Mr. Nixon came to Chico as one who had seen Communism firsthand in the world. Tracing his political career from his days as a member of the House Committee on Un-American Activities ("my work was often unpopular") to his "kitchen debate" with Premier Khrushchev, he vowed to combat "the grave dangers of Communism in California."

In detail, the anti-Communist platform Mr. Nixon outlined was moderate enough, and familiar: a "three-pronged" program of "investigation, legislation and education," and a public school "program of indoctrination" which would provide California with "the best Communist control of any state in the United States." He was several times halted by applause and at the end was awarded a considerable ovation.

Mr. Nixon linked Communism to "big government," and "big government," in turn, to the administration of Governor Brown. It was a syllogism I was left to complete for myself: Governor Brown's administration was Communistic. Mr. Nixon—not having quite said it, but only implied it—remained free of responsibility for the syllogism. His call for "individualism—the spirit of the real West"—held out the prospect of a return to thrift, economy, frugality, welfare reductions "across the board." It was a nostalgic voyage I would eagerly undertake, if only it were possible, a return to an age when life was simple, easy, pure—when everybody knew the good guys from the bad guys.

Mr. Nixon flew out of Chico. On the plane I sat drinking coffee with Mrs. Nixon, for whom the enthusiasm of the audience had been exhilarating. "Wasn't that exciting?" she said. "It was just like a revival meeting."

Had Governor Brown or Mr. Nixon more accurately read the California heart? Bread and butter and lettuce and water on one hand, individualism and a revival spirit on the other—broadly outlined, these were the vital forces the candidates descried.

California's stance on Nov. 6 might challenge any future historian to explain American development. Ancient in her heart, tomorrow first in population, dual in character, part matter, part spirit, and all vital force, California was a replica of the America that had swarmed into her. Where now would history lead her?

Though I had at one point half hoped to go unnoticed, I now half feared that that would be the fact. My weeks of labor, packed into two facing pages, had a cramped, condensed appearance, jammed up, set in type which at first appeared to me very small, although as my satisfaction with the article increased, the size of the type also increased. As I had been shocked by the transition of my manuscript to Working Draft, so was I now shocked again by the transition of Working Draft to printed page. I was certain that terrible cuts had been made, a willful destruction wrought upon my spirit. Yet nothing essential had been altered.

I knew how much less my article was than it might

have been. My leisurely historian was dead, nothing of him remaining but the phrase "explain American development" in the final paragraph. And I was dead with him, my grave marked by the word "Continued" at the end of my article, by which *Life* meant that *it* continued—*they* continued. I had become merged with *Life*, buried among its pages, treated not as myself but as a continuity, cruel liberties taken even with my age, which was given as forty, though I was still thirty-nine. (I am forty *now*.)

Lacking the virtues of my Frost-Sandburg article, it failed even to compensate with judgment. Where was the judgment? Whom did the writer favor for governor? Whom was he *for*? Rereading the article, I received the impression, from a single paragraph near the end, that the writer was trying to express timid, oblique reservations about Mr. Nixon's logic, but there was nothing thumping about those reservations, nothing hard-hitting, as if the writer, out of a hesitation to guide me, were withholding his own judgment. He failed to satisfy my prejudices.

I bought twelve copies and went into the street, self-conscious, expecting at any moment to be apprehended for a malfeasance soon to be discovered, a transgression not quite punishable yet not quite honorable, not something wicked but nevertheless an offense against decency, something not to be proud of. My friends would cluck and say, "He ought to be ashamed."

I had not gone far enough. I had muffed my chance at social criticism. The only word from what *Life* called "the lonely minority" came in the form of an article by a Hollywood writer, photographed on the diving board of his swimming pool, who complained of traffic jams and too much social life. Trouble was dismissed as if it were a joke—Mr. Nixon's cartoons on the wall of his alcove. The nearest the California Issue approached to the reality of human discomfort were the two facing pages purchased by Metropolitan Life and offering free pamphlets entitled "Your Heart," "Facts About Cancer," "Weight Control," "When Our Parents Get Old," "Alcoholism," and "Stress."

My friend The Real Mark was intensely critical of me, and for a while I thought he was justified. I read my article over and over again, often sneaking up upon it, as if I were a common reader, hoping each time that the prejudices of the writer might come on stronger. But I could never feel that my partisanship was clear. If I had struck a blow, it was soft. It was not nearly what I felt, nor what I knew. I had been too fair.

That this had been my intention was at first no consolation. The triumph of my mind over itself was a distinctly subordinate issue when matched against the possibility of Mr. Nixon's becoming governor of California.

At mid-October the public-opinion polls showed the candidates running even, and I who had thrown away my opportunities began to work in smaller ways: I wore buttons and pins saying PAT BROWN FOR ME on all my suits; I displayed a large BROWN FOR GOVERNOR poster in a second-floor window visible to all that portion of mankind who should be traveling down Seward Street; I affixed pro-

Brown stickers to the bumpers of my Toyopet, both front and rear; I urged everybody I met to vote for him; and I signed newspaper advertisements in his behalf.

And then it was that I became aware of my magnification. The tenfold magnification of the Working Draft was now the 1,400,000-fold magnification of the *Life* article, whose phrases began coming home to me. I read them in the newspapers, in the press releases still coming to me from my various liaisons; I heard them on radio, and saw them, so to speak, in the mouths of commentators on television. To commentators writing or speaking from the East, I seemed to be an expert, upon the grounds that I was a Californian, was *there*. On the other hand, California writers and editors, mistrusting *Life* for its eastern origins, but respecting it for the same reasons, found in my article phrases convenient to describe feelings forming in themselves.

Apparently it struck people as an honest report, fair— "a fair summary," a Republican neighbor told me—somehow accurate in its emotion, somehow to be trusted, somehow inviting confidence, somehow as if its author, having fought hard against his passion, deserved to be listened to with particular attention. Its author (though declining) was flattered to be invited to appear on nonpartisan radio and television programs, in the role of expert.

But I was no expert. I had been, above all, a writer, and that had been my power. "Sometimes it's a hate," said Robert Frost, "somebody I hate, somebody I've argued with makes me write a poem." But then, said Frost, you put your hate away, and you go to your discipline. I had begun in hatred. "Your first discipline is your vocabulary; then your grammar and your punctuation, you see. Then, in your exuberance and bounding energy you say you're going to add to that. Then you add rhyme and meter. And your delight is in *that* power." So Frost told me, when I went to him for *Life;* and I tried, by putting off hatred and going to my discipline, to produce an article above prejudice and therefore believable because it wasn't wild, like prejudice; it wasn't dirty; it didn't depend upon loaded adjectives; it had shed hatred, using not hatred but the power beneath. It must have been convincing, for it touched editors and must have touched beyond, and must have been responsible along with a good many other things, not the least of which were the record and the person of the Governor, for the turning of the tide.

Ten days before Election Day, as suddenly as it had ascended, my panic subsided, and I knew the Governor would win. It was no feat—I claim no powers of political prophecy—it was only the mind of Mr. Nixon giving itself to me for the last time: his projections, his accusations against the Governor; the Governor was growing frightened now, said Mr. Nixon; the Governor had seen private polls . . . the Governor would become desperate . . . the Governor would engage in a smear campaign. Translated, it was Mr. Nixon's own desperation, according to that process I had observed, his meager self-knowledge, that collapse of control whereby we foist upon our enemies our own motives and passions.

Five days later I was reassured, though not necessarily surprised, by the contents of a letter I received from John

McDonald, whom I had met upon my first visit to the Governor's headquarters:

Many thanks for calling to my attention the faculty ad on Nixon and academic freedom. As you may have seen, The Examiner used the story on page one today.

I think we're going to win a close election. If we do, and it is close, your LIFE story will have played a major part.

Anyway, we'll know pretty soon.

Best regards,

JACK

But then it wasn't even close, really, and it is hard to know what we know.

Two days after Mr. Nixon's last un-election the *New York Times* Western Edition carried his photograph opposite a photograph of Mrs. Eleanor Roosevelt, who had died the night before. She was one of those "woolly-heads" denounced by Mr. Nixon in his Farewell Address.

Her vision of the end, whatever its limitations, arose from charity and warmth. It had not been her career but her life. Since such a vision is unattainable within a lifetime, the life ends, the vision lives.

But what vision of life has Mr. Nixon left with us?

My friend The Real Mark, confessing at last that assassination would have been foolish and wasteful, suggested that we write Mr. Nixon "a real gloating letter": *Dear Mr. Nixon, We are great fans of yours and followed your campaign for governor until our subscription lapsed. Can you tell us how it came out?* . . . But we never wrote it, or wrote anything to him.

Mark The Glove Boy, with the feeling that he had left his mark on the United States, as he had left it long ago on the Village of Port Chester, clung to his classroom, where he continues to the present time, sailing with Mark Twain on the Mississippi, theorizing with Turner, going forward with his own education and with the education of others—educating, not indoctrinating—confident that good ideas will make their way in time so long as he is let alone by every governor of California, vigilant but relatively unworried, feeling rather better than he had felt in October, 1962, about the future of the state, and pleased with himself, too, as if by being good he had done well, or witnessed in some way something like the triumph of virtue in a naughty world.